BLUE
GUITAR

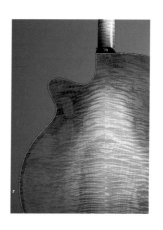

BLUE
GUITAR

WRITTEN BY KEN VOSE

PHOTOGRAPHY BY LESLIE JEAN-BART

FOREWORD BY GEORGE BENSON

CHRONICLE BOOKS

SAN FRANCISCO

DEDICATION

For Chris—Without you, I'd be the man with the blues.

Selection from *On Being Blue* by William Gass, copyright © 1976
by William Gass, reprinted by permission of David R. Godine, Publisher.

Selections from "Man with the Blue Guitar" from *Collected Poems*
by Wallace Stevens, copyright © 1936 by Wallace Stevens and renewed
1964 by Holly Stevens. Reprinted by permission of Alfred A. Knopf, Inc.

Text copyright © 1998 by Ken Vose
Photography copyright © 1998 by Leslie Jean-Bart

Printed in Hong Kong.

Library of Congress Cataloging-in-Publication Data:

Vose, Ken.
Blue Guitar / text Ken Vose; original photography by Leslie Jean-Bart;
foreword by George Benson
p. cm.
Includes bibliographical references.
ISBN 0-8118-1912-4
1. Guitar I. Jean-Bart, Leslie.
ML1015.G9V67 1998
787.87'192'2—dc21   97-25672
                         CIP

Cover and book design: WORKSIGHT

Front cover photographs: D'AQUISTO CENTURA DELUXE

Case wrap art: COPYRIGHT © 1994, ROBERT BENEDETTO

Distributed in Canada by Raincoast Books,
8680 Cambie Street Vancouver BC V6P 6M9

10 9 8 7 6 5 4 3 2 1

Chronicle Books 85 Second Street San Francisco, CA 94105

Web Site: www.chronbooks.com

ACKNOWLEDGMENTS

My heartfelt thanks to Scott Chinery, without whose vision and love of the archtop there would have been no Blue Guitars; Mike Carey, who always managed to pull the rabbit out of the hat on time; Leslie Jean-Bart, each of whose pictures is indeed worth all those words; Chris Tomasino, my peerless agent; George Benson; Steve Howe; Martin Taylor; Walter Carter; Larry Acunto; Nick Carella; Nion McEvoy, Christina Wilson, Michael Carabetta, David Featherstone, and the staff of Chronicle Books; Randall Kremer and Gary Sturm of the Smithsonian Institution; Marvin Shanken, Gordon Mott, Terry Fagan, Bruce Goldman, and the rest of the crew at *Cigar Aficionado* magazine; and, finally, all of the luthiers who took time out of their busy schedules to answer my endless questions.

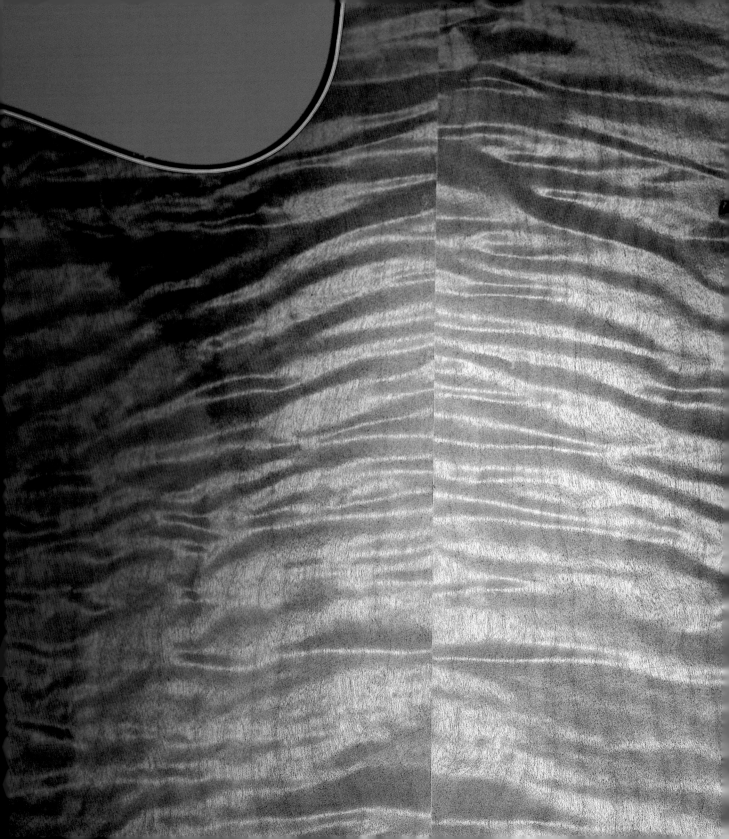

Table of Contents

FOREWORD

BY GEORGE BENSON

I grew up in a house without electricity. It wasn't until I was seven years old that my mother, stepfather, and I moved into a place with electric lights. Well, almost, since the people who had been there before stole all the light bulbs. It was that first day in that house that I became a guitar player.

My stepfather had gone down to the pawnshop and gotten his amplifier out. Here we were, just moving in at twilight, with no furniture yet; you could barely see in the room. He went and got himself a chair. He put the amplifier on one side of the room, plugged the guitar in, and the most amazing thing happened. I was sitting on the floor watching him playing this Epiphone Emperor archtop, and I could hear the sound coming out of a box on the other side of the room. It was like a miracle. I'm sitting there thinking about all that sound going through that skinny wire, like it was some sort of hollow tube. From that moment on, I was fascinated by the acoustic electric guitar. Not just the guitar itself, the acoustic electric guitar.

When my stepfather finished, he put the guitar down on the chair; and as he walked out of the room he said, "I don't want you to touch that." Well, that was the worst thing he could have said. As soon as he was gone, I tried to hit the three notes that used to be the signature of NBC on the radio. I hit the first two, and just as I hit the third one he came back into the room, looked at me, and said, "Now you're gonna have to learn to play it." And that was the beginning.

My stepfather was a nut for Charlie Christian. His were about the only records he played—Charlie Christian with Benny Goodman. I knew all of Charlie Christian's solos by heart. It was a great foundation for me, because if things didn't measure up to that, they didn't appeal to me at all. Then I heard Oscar Moore, who played with Nat King Cole. He had the most beautiful guitar sound. Finally, in my teens, I started to listen to Kenny Burrell and of course, Wes Montgomery. They all played amplified acoustic archtop guitars, just as the best of today's younger players are looking to the archtop to get the sound they want. The archtop is a totally unique guitar whose sound has not been duplicated by any other instrument.

I have a D'Aquisto Solo that Jimmy originally built for Earl Klugh. Jimmy knew that the instrument Earl had been playing didn't really fit his style—he was trying to play jazz and blues on a flat-top. So Jimmy designed a guitar to duplicate the sound that would match the concept Earl had in his head. I used the D'Aquisto on my last album, and when I played it in the studio the producer said, "Man, what kind of guitar is that?"

I have a couple of D'Angelico New Yorkers, one of which D'Aquisto worked on when he was in John D'Angelico's shop. I think that Jimmy D'Aquisto inspired all of today's luthiers; D'Angelico did too, but I believe that Jimmy eventually surpassed D'Angelico. His instruments are the finest I've ever played, and they just keep on getting better and better. The problem with getting Jimmy to make you a guitar was the time involved—it took about five years. That's why I never had him make me one. I knew I would have worried him to death. He offered to make me one years ago, but I said, "Jimmy, I'd rather stay friends with you."

Once, when I was in Steve Grimes's [a Blue Guitar luthier] workshop, I asked him what he had for sale, and he said, "Well, you know I don't really like to sell my guitars." They were his babies just like D'Aquisto and his guitars. That's probably why it takes so long to get a guitar from a luthier; they just don't want to let go of them. All kidding aside, working with a luthier to get an instrument that's tailored to your body and your playing style is worth the wait.

For guitar makers—and players—this book and the exhibit of the Blue Guitars at the Smithsonian Institution really mean a lot. For one thing, they tell the story from the luthiers' point of view. They also let people know about Scott Chinery, who cared enough to give the luthiers the recognition that they deserve.

All kidding aside, working with a luthier to get an instrument that's tailored to your body and your playing style is worth the wait.

PREFACE

A collection of guitars might be an historical survey of guitar making, or it might document the state-of-the-art of guitars and guitar playing. But a collection of blue guitars is more a statement about our perceptions of color than it is a representation of musical instruments. Yes, the Blue Guitars are indeed musical instruments, but their unusual color makes them transcend their function and broadens our interpretation of what they are.

The Blue Guitars of the Chinery Collection are a tribute to all contemporary musical instrument makers. They are a reminder that old-world traditions continue to be expressed through individual craftsmanship and that the art of lutherie is thriving in our contemporary society. But because they are a tribute to the state of guitar making and a link in the chain of craft tradition, they are more than just guitars. Blue guitars become sculpture. They break through traditional barriers and, perceived as artworks, open doorways to surreal imagination.

A blue guitar says much about the cultural importance of color. Our experience with guitars tells us they are traditionally varnished in hues of brown or yellow. Encountering a blue guitar in our daily lives is as unexpected as seeing a green violin. While the shapes are easily recognized, the unusual colors suggest these guitars have another meaning. The color triggers reinterpretation of what they are. And leads us to wonder, a blue guitar? How bizarre.

Gary Sturm
Division of Cultural History
Smithsonian Institution

INTRODUCTION

PART I—THE LUTHIER LINE:
MASTER BUILDERS FROM STAUFFER TO D'ANGELICO

T he archtop guitar is a relatively recent addition to the world of fretted instruments. Throughout the first hundred years of the guitar's development, it has been dominated by a succession of strong-willed, idiosyncratic artisans whose legacy of craftsmanship and beauty has served both to inspire and challenge the following generations.

The luthiers who made the Blue Guitars are continuing a tradition that began in Spain in the early sixteenth century and continued its development in France, Italy, Austria, and, finally, America, where more than fourteen million players have made the guitar the most popular of all musical instruments.

The Blue Guitar project pays homage to all of these great luthiers, particularly the late Jimmy D'Aquisto, in whose memory it was conceived.

From its appearance in the mid-sixteenth century to the development of Orville Gibson's first carved-top instruments in the late 1800s, the guitar underwent a steady evolutionary process. Probably evolving from the lute, it quickly overtook its predecessors. This was due, at least in part, to the ease with which it could be mastered; a point made none too subtly by William Turner in 1697.

Johan Stauffer guitar, circa 1820

"The fine easie Ghittar, whose performance is soon gained, at least after the brushing way, hath at this present time over-topt the nobler lute."

In Renaissance Spain, the *vihuela*, another popular precursor to the guitar, also found itself under siege.

"Since guitars were invented, those who devote themselves to a study of the vihuela are small in number. It has been a great loss, as all kinds of plucked music could be played on it: but now the guitar is no more than a cow-bell, so easy to play, especially rasgueado [strumming], there is not a stable lad who is not a musician on the guitar." Don Sebastian Covarrubias Orozco, 1611

These early instruments had four "courses" of strings; in each course, single, double, or triple strings were tuned an octave apart or in unison for added volume and fuller sounding chords. The five-course guitar followed soon after and, finally, around 1775, the first instruments with six single strings appeared. There were other advances in the period, but the guitar, now featuring the flat back and top that are still in use today, basically was fully formed by the early 1800s.

Although the great Italian violin maker Antonio Stradivari made a few guitars in the late 1600s, Johann Stauffer, who began making guitars in Vienna in about 1800, was the first undisputed master of the instrument.

Many twentieth-century innovations can be traced back to Stauffer's workshop, including the scroll-shaped peghead with the tuners on one side, the detachable neck, the raised fingerboard, and the first "signature" model guitars endorsed and autographed by famous artists of the day.

Unfortunately, innovation has never guaranteed success, and Stauffer, who stopped making guitars in order to produce violins, died in the poorhouse in 1853.

"There is not a stable lad who is not a musician on the guitar."

One of Stauffer's employees, a shop foreman named Christian Friedrich Martin, emigrated to the United States in 1833. Martin pioneered the *X*-braced top, in which two diagonal braces inside the guitar cross below the soundhole.

He also promoted the use of steel strings instead of the traditional gut versions, changing the sound of the instrument and greatly increasing its volume. The firm that C. F. Martin founded is still in the guitar business and still run by a C. F. Martin (the fourth).

The inability of the flat-top guitar to project its sound delayed its acceptance by composers and many members of the music establishment, as can be seen in the following two extracts from *The Giulianiad*, an 1830s British periodical devoted to the guitar. First, this less than rave review.

"Duets for guitars!—what a feast for those who delectate in congregated nasal twangs! It is not amiss as a companion to the dessert, to assist the voice in a romance, or in an unpretending arietta. But give to it brilliant compositions, requiring the execution of a violinist, and suited, so far as manner is concerned, to the concert room, it then becomes as ineffective as a piping bullfinch perched on a trombone in the midst of a military band."

A slightly more sympathetic point of view could be found in a second article, titled "On Public Performance on the Guitar."

C. F. Martin guitar, circa 1840

"People hearing a performance on the guitar in a large room, for the first time, are generally disappointed. The reason is obvious: not taking into consideration the limited powers of the instrument, so far as loudness is concerned, they misdirect their attention from the merits of the instrument, and fix it on its want of power, which is its greatest defect."

Orville H. Gibson, who was born in Chateaugay, New York, in 1856, would correct these presumed shortcomings. While still a young man, he relocated to Kalamazoo, Michigan, where he worked in various clerking and restaurant jobs until he established himself as a maker of violins and mandolins sometime in the mid-1890s.

If America was known for any type of musical instrument in the later part of the nineteenth century, it was the banjo, with its thousand or more manufacturers and distributors.

Popular since the 1840s, the banjo was now about to be replaced in the parlors and concert halls by another very distinctive sounding instrument, the mandolin.

Long a favorite in Italy, Neopolitan mandolins were first seen in America at least a decade before the signing of the Declaration of Independence; but it wasn't until a troupe of Spanish musicians playing their local version of the instrument, the *bandurria,* appeared in New York in 1880 that the mandolin "craze" began. Before long, mandolin orchestras were picking away from coast to coast.

The time had arrived for Orville Gibson to make his mark by, in the words of Gibson historian Walter Carter, *"building musical instruments that the world did not know it needed."*

Unlike other historically famous luthiers, Gibson didn't just refine previous construction techniques, he used them to create a new type of instrument altogether. His mandolins, and later, guitars, featured a violin-style, carved-top soundboard that arched upward, away from the back and sides. The backs of the instruments, made from a single piece of wood, were carved on the inside. The side rims also were carved from a solid block of wood.

If there is any doubt that Gibson thought his instruments were superior, one has only to read his 1895 patent application:

"Every portion of the woody structure seems to be alive with emphatic sound at every touch of the instrument—a character and quality of sound entirely new to this class of musical instruments, and which cannot be imparted to others by a description in words."

But words must have done the trick, since his patent was granted on February 1, 1898.

(left to right) Orville Gibson carved-top guitar, circa 1898; 1924 Gibson/Lloyd Loar L=5; 1955 Stromberg Master 400

In 1902, Gibson and five good citizens of Kalamazoo with some ready cash signed an agreement to form a *"Partnership Association Limited...for the purpose of manufacturing, selling, and dealing in guitars, mandolins, mandolas, violins, lutes, and all other kinds of stringed instruments."* For a fee of $2,500, Orville assigned the Gibson Mandolin-Guitar Mfg. Co. his patent and the use of his name, and he became a consultant to the new entity. Though he would receive some royalties, he never actually became a partner in the company that bore his name. In fact, within a year he had sold the only sixty shares of company stock he owned to a saloon keeper for $600.

Although Gibson died in Odgensburg, New York, in 1918, after years of illness, he lived long enough to see his carved-top concept revolutionize the mandolin business. Within a decade of his death, the large-body archtop—with the penetrating sound that Gibson had pioneered—would become the standard guitar of the big band era.

The next master luthier on the fretted-instrument scene was a young mandolin player named Lloyd Allayre Loar. Born in Cropsy, Illinois, in 1886, he made his reputation as a performer before going to work for the Gibson Company as a consultant in 1919. Loar refined Orville Gibson's original concepts and designed a group of instruments known as the "Master Models." The Master Model family consisted of an F-5 mandolin, H-5 mandola, K-5 mandocello, and L-5 guitar. All of the instruments featured violin-style *f*-holes rather than the round or oval shapes commonly used. He also "tuned" the woods used in the instruments in order to give them acoustically perfect properties.

A few of John D'Angelico's 1164 instruments

Loar left Gibson in 1924 to pursue other interests, which included the design of electric pickup amplification systems and keyboard instruments.

Another early archtop builder, Elmer Stromberg, was famous among jazz players of the 1930s, 1940s, and 1950s for his huge nineteen-inch Master 400, which had a sound that could cut through the loudest horn sections. The Master 400s were, according to guitar expert George Gruhn, *"the loudest guitars in creation."*

Born in Chelsea, Massachusetts, in 1895, Stromberg apprenticed with his father, Charles, who was also a luthier. By the time he was fifteen, the two had begun building instruments together.

Stromberg's guitars were known for the quality of the wood used in their construction; according to some who knew him, it was often salvaged from old houses that were being torn down. He had a reputation for doing things his own way when it came to size, bracing, and proper tone; his single diagonal top brace instead of the standard *X* is but one example. The 640 or so archtops Stromberg made before his death in 1955 are highly prized by both players and collectors.

Our final master of the archtop, the man who taught the craft to Jimmy D'Aquisto and paved the way for today's crop of talented luthiers, was John D'Angelico.

Born in New York in 1905, D'Angelico apprenticed with his uncle making violins, mandolins, and flat-top guitars. He set up shop on his own in 1932 to make large-body archtops. His top-of-the-line model, the New Yorker, introduced in 1936, was almost identical in size to the eighteen-inch Gibson Super 400, which had gone on sale two years earlier. Demand for his instruments grew over the years, and by the time of his death in 1964, he had hand-made a total of 1,164 guitars.

Beginning in 1952, D'Angelico first taught and then worked alongside the luthier whose instruments would ultimately inspire the Blue Guitar Project, Jimmy D'Aquisto.

PART II—THE BIRTH OF THE BLUES

Many of us collect things. Pens, hats, baseball cards, salt and pepper shakers— things. Scott Chinery collects guitars. Lots of guitars. At last count, he had more than a thousand of them and not one run-of-the-mill. These instruments are among the most important guitars ever made.

When you collect on such a vast scale, you invariably run into the problem of what to do once you've acquired the best examples of everything available in the marketplace. For some, the answer lies in starting over, collecting something completely different. For Chinery, the solution was to create something new and thoroughly unique, the Blue Guitars. These guitars are not only the crown jewels of an already extraordinary collection, they are also an homage to a man considered to be America's greatest luthier ever, Jimmy D'Aquisto.

Not long before his death in 1995, D'Aquisto crafted an eighteen-inch Centura Deluxe archtop for the Chinery Collection. Finished in a bold blue sunburst, it would become the inspiration for the Blue

Guitar Project and for the luthiers selected to participate. As Chinery recalled:

"During the spring of 1995, I saw the archtop guitar hitting a peak in terms of quality and diversity. There were more talented luthiers making instruments than at any other time in history, more than one hundred in North America alone.

"I had often thought it would be neat to get all of the great portrait painters together to interpret the same subject and then see the differences among them. So that's what I set out to do with the Blue Guitars. I planned to get all the greatest builders and have them interpret the same guitar, an eighteen-inch archtop, in the same color blue that Jimmy had used.

"When I put together the list of possible luthiers I wanted to represent the whole spectrum of style and price, say from $3,500 to $35,000. All of these great luthiers saw this as a friendly competition. As a result, they went beyond anything they'd ever done and we ended up with a collection of the greatest archtop guitars ever made."

"BLUE BEING BLUE" by Leslie Jean-Bart

Why blue? For Chinery, the answer is somewhat complex.

"The color was chosen before I ever conceived the idea of the Blue Guitars. Jimmy D'Aquisto and I were discussing where the archtop was going. We both had very definite feelings that the archtop was more suited to many types of music than the flat-top. We wanted to build a modern archtop that embodied that concept, and one of the considerations was aesthetics. We started discussing colors. We considered purple and even red, but for some reason blue just seemed the perfect color to jolt people out the old, staid, traditional way of looking at the archtop."

Each of the Blue Guitars features the work of one of the world's best archtop guitar makers. Every luthier was presented with the same task: Make an eighteen-inch-wide acoustic archtop guitar; make it as traditional or as far out as your imagination can take you; make it any way you want, as long as you make it blue.

Although each luthier used identical Ultra Blue Penetrating Stain #M 520, from Mohawk Finishing Products in Amsterdam, New York, the end results were anything but standardized. There's probably not a shade of blue that can't be found somewhere on one of these guitars.

A more profound reason for selecting the color blue can be found in philosopher William Gass's extraordinary book, *On Being Blue: A Philosophical Inquiry.* "Of the colors, blue and green have the greatest emotional range. Sad reds and melancholy yellows are difficult to turn up. Among the ancient elements, blue occurs everywhere: in ice and water, in the flame as purely as the flower, overhead and inside caves, covering fruit and oozing out of clay. Although green enlivens the earth and mixes in the ocean, and we find it, copperish, in fire, green air, green skies, are rare. Gray and brown are widely distributed, but there are no joyful swatches of either, or of any exuberant black, sullen pink, or acquiescent orange. Blue is therefore most suitable as the color of interior life. Whether slick light sharp high bright thin quick sour new and cool or low deep sweet thick dark soft slow smooth heavy old and warm: blue moves easily among them all, and all profoundly qualify our states of feeling."

These beautiful blue creations echo, in wood, steel, silver, gold, abalone, and pearl, the same sense of wonder that Gass evokes with his eloquent words.

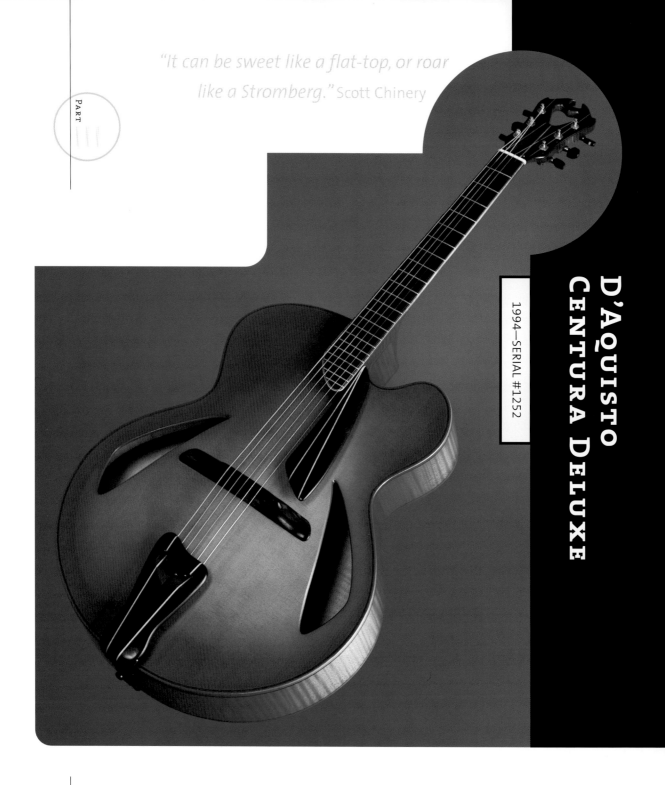

"It can be sweet like a flat-top, or roar like a Stromberg." Scott Chinery

1994—SERIAL #1252

D'AQUISTO
CENTURA DELUXE

PART III—JIMMY D'AQUISTO

I n 1952, seventeen-year-old James L. D'Aquisto, already an accomplished jazz guitarist, apprenticed himself to legendary archtop builder John D'Angelico. Jimmy soon graduated from sweeping up the shop and running errands to working on the guitars themselves. As D'Aquisto's skills increased, D'Angelico, a lifelong bachelor,

D'Angelico Teardrop New Yorker

began to see him as the son he'd never had. Slowly, this great archtop guitar maker's secrets were passed to the next generation.

In 1960, D'Angelico suffered what would be the first of a series of heart attacks that would eventually claim his life. Over the next four years, D'Aquisto became the older man's hands, completing guitar after guitar under D'Angelico's watchful eye. John D'Angelico died at age fifty-nine on September 1, 1964, leaving behind a legacy of beautifully made archtop guitars. One of them, the 1957 Teardrop New Yorker, is generally considered to be the most valuable guitar in the world.

For Jimmy D'Aquisto, who had been working with D'Angelico for twelve years, his mentor's death resulted in unanticipated legal problems and an eventual change in direction. The D'Angelico name became the property of the D'Angelico String Company, and after a short stint making guitars under the D'Angelico name, D'Aquisto set out on his own.

After his own untimely death (like D'Angelico, at age fifty-nine) D'Aquisto was acknowledged as the premiere archtop maker of our time. He also made a small number of flat-tops and mandolins, and he designed guitars for Fender and for Hagstrom, a Swedish manufacturer.

While Jimmy had no single apprentice to whom he passed on his remarkable skills, he did occasionally allow other makers who met his high standards to work with him in his Long Island studio. One of them, Canadian luthier Linda Manzer, recalls the experience.

(top to bottom)
Jimmy D'Aquisto in his workshop, 1983
Linda Manzer at D'Aquisto's workbench, 1983
Jimmy D'Aquisto, 1983

"I was surprised and delighted to receive an unexpected phone call from D'Aquisto in 1982 inviting me to visit his workshop. He was a living legend I had only read about in books.

"He loved talking to other guitar makers about the archtop guitar, because he truly believed that it was the most versatile of all guitars and could do anything a player could want, if it was adjusted properly. He invited me to learn to build archtops with him during the winter of 1983–84.

"Working with him was an exhausting but magical experience. Although he was a man who loved lively discussion—very lively at times—sometimes he said more with his silence. I would watch him as he'd feel the weight and texture of each piece of wood before he would even tap it. After he felt acquainted with the wood, he'd silently make a decision about how it would interact with the other woods. Then the work began. As he carved the tops and backs, he would work the wood with

Linda Manzer

confidence. One always had the feeling he knew exactly where he was going with each guitar. He had what can only be described as a 'special touch' for the wood. He seemed to sense the characteristics of each piece, deciding how it could best be used in his guitar.

"He said that he felt very restricted in his early years by traditional archtop design, that he felt he didn't have any room to experiment. He said to me, 'You are so lucky. You can do anything you want; everyone expects me to build what I always build.' But his mind was filled with ideas and designs. In his last years, he finally had the chance to do the experimentation he had always wanted to do. With such incredible guitars as the Classic, the Solo, the Centura, and the Avant Garde, and finally his peek into the future with the Advance, one had the feeling he was just getting started. We will never know what else would have been created from his hands and heart. However, he has left us a wonderful legacy and a truly inspired path to follow.

"He once told me that it was important to put all your feelings and emotions into your work, good or bad.

Archtop building was the essence of his life. He lived for and dreamed about his guitars. It's possible to believe that a little bit of his soul went into each of those guitars."

Perhaps it's that "little bit of his soul" that makes D'Aquisto's Centura Deluxe stand out, even in the rarified company of its fellow Blue Guitars. Scott Chinery certainly feels it.

"The D'Aquisto has all of the elements that make you want to play it and play it. And the more you play it, the more you love it; the more you're intrigued by the complexity and depth of it. *It keeps drawing you back, over and over again.*"

"When Scott first told me about The Blue Guitar Project, I thought it was one of the most way-out ideas I'd ever heard of. Then, when I saw them all standing up there on display, it was sensational—unlike anything else in the world.

"These guitars salute Jimmy, and they also take his work and build on it. He was a very adventurous idea man, and by his example he gave a lot of other makers the idea they they could try something different. This collection is a tremendous tribute to him."

Steve Howe

The Blue Guitar Project luthiers are taking this long tradition of loving craftsmanship and carrying it into the future. A future where one of them might well become to the next generation what D'Angelico and D'Aquisto were to them.

The work of these luthiers is divided into two categories —classicist and modernist. This division is not based on the way the guitars are made, or even necessarily on the way they sound. Each represents a different philosophical attitude regarding the archtop and its place in the contemporary music scene.

At its most basic, the classicist believes the contemporary archtop should be a refinement of all the best that has gone before, while the modernist often thinks more in terms of changes that will make the instrument more versatile.

Although groupings of this sort are arbitrary and inevitably overlap, they serve a purpose; they remind us that ideals, commitment, and passion are as much a part of each guitar as abalone, ebony, and aged rosewood.

"BLUES FOR JIMMY" by Leslie Jean-Bart

"BLUETTE" by Leslie Jean-Bart

THE CLASSICISTS

The man bent over his guitar,

A shearsman of sorts. The day was green.

They said, "You have a blue guitar,

You do not play things as they are."

The man replied, "Things as they are

Are changed upon the blue guitar."

And they said then, "But play, you must,

A tune beyond us, yet ourselves,

A tune upon the blue guitar

Of things exactly as they are."

Excerpt from "Man with the Blue Guitar," by Wallace Stevens

"There is a tremendous amount of artistry in the sound; a consistent balance, very defined." Steve Howe

1996—SERIAL #37996

LA CREMONA AZZURRA
(THE BLUE CREMONA)

ROBERT BENEDETTO

With over thirty years' experience and more than 650 musical instruments to his credit, including 400 archtops, Bob Benedetto is one of the most accomplished and respected of the current crop of top luthiers.

Born in the Bronx, New York, in 1946 into a family of woodworking craftsmen and musicians, Benedetto began playing the guitar professionally at thirteen and building archtops at twenty-one.

"My father and grandfather were master cabinetmakers. Antonino, my grandfather, was employed by the Steinway Company as an expert polisher and woodcarver—he carved the piano's lion legs. As with many typical Italian families, on weekends we would gather to eat, sing, and play music, so I grew up around the guitar and the mandolin.

"I was eleven when I really discovered the archtop guitar. While I learned woodworking from my father, it was my Uncle Mike who had a beautiful Gretsch archtop and showed me how it worked; the bracings, the vibrations of the top, how the sound comes out the f- holes, etcetera.

"From that point, I daydreamed constantly about archtops. They're my lifetime passion and my focus. No one ever became a master maker by making a few of this or that. I feel you have to make many archtops, over and over, before you can begin to understand the subtle nuances of the instrument."

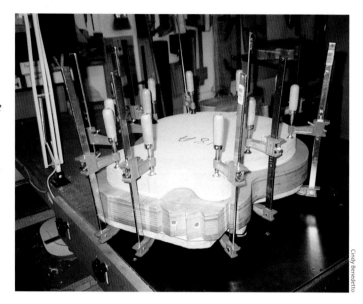

Cindy Benedetto

Benedetto's first attempts at what would become his life's work were duly noted by the rest of the family.

"I really didn't know where to get the wood for the first few I made, so I cut up the thirty-year-old maple kitchen table and used that for several guitar necks. I even cut up my sister's bed while she was away before I finally started buying wood commercially. Now I have a tremendous inventory of American and European woods."

The creation of the Blue Cremona gave Benedetto the chance to combine innovation and tradition in a single instrument, and it took substantially more time to build than what is normally scheduled for an archtop.

"To begin with, I had to think about it a lot. I used the best European cello wood—it's very old. It's a very fine tone wood supplied by family businesses that are generations old; the same type of wood that Stradivari and all the other great instrument makers from centuries ago used."

A veteran innovator, Benedetto stripped away unnecessary inlays and bindings in a custom instrument he made for jazz guitarist Chuck Wayne in 1982. Unique at the time, the idea inspired other makers, including D'Aquisto. This technique would be put to expert use on the Blue Cremona.

"To assure a more acoustically pure instrument, with increased volume as well as tone, the guitar is void of binding and utilizes violin-inspired lightweight construction."

Benedetto is one of the few guitar makers who also makes violins; he devoted much of the mid-1980s to the study of violin lutherie.

"Although I never wanted to make anything but the archtop, there was one exception and that was the violin. Making violins has helped me tremendously in honing my guitar-making skills, particularly regarding the tuning of the top and back plates. Unlike the guitar, subjectivity in sound is virtually nonexistent with a violin. It's either right or it's wrong."

Robert Benedetto signs
the back of his guitar

The Blue Cremona features Benedetto's trademark minimalist abalone inlays throughout, and an unusual use of black fittings to complete the overall dark motif.

The fingerboard, bridge, truss-rod cover, nut, and fingerrest are all sculpted of select solid ebony, and the headstock is veneered with exotic burl. Perhaps the instrument's most striking features are the unique floral clustered sound openings instead of the traditional oval or *f*-holes.

"The sound openings are an unusual design and placed in an unusual location. This had to be considered when I was carving and tuning the woods and the bracing inside, which act as tone bars distributing the vibrations from the strings to the top. All of this maximizes the end result— a loud, strongly-voiced, and well-balanced instrument."

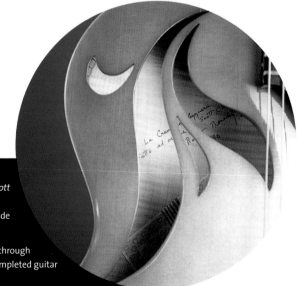

*La Cremona Azzurra
fatto ad ordine per Scott
Chinery* (the Blue
Cremona custom-made
for Scott Chinery)

The inscription seen through
soundholes of the completed guitar

The idea for one innovative feature to be found on the Blue Cremona originated with the man who commissioned it:

"I gave directions to several of the luthiers that I wanted to vent some of the sound toward the player. When you're playing, you can't really appreciate the quality of the tone because the traditional guitar projects the sound forward toward the audience. Bob created an incredible design for this both acoustically and aesthetically. When I look at this guitar, it doesn't look like somebody built it—

it looks like it was born."

Benedetto with second-generation jazz guitarist, John Pizzarelli

Cindy Benedetto

"A powerful guitar with great tonal qualities." Scott Chinery

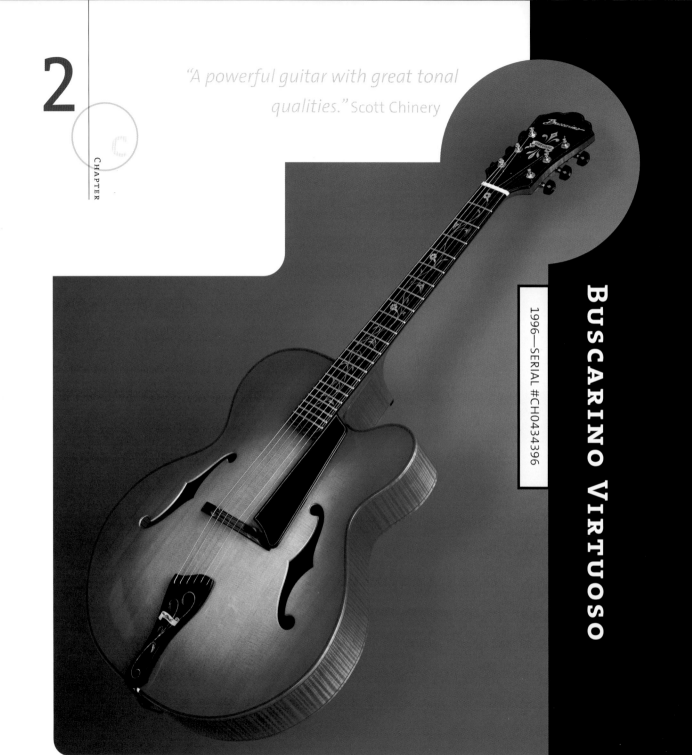

BUSCARINO VIRTUOSO

John Buscarino

Alphabetical placement notwithstanding, the fact that Buscarino follows Benedetto could not be more appropriate, because John Buscarino studied for two years with Bob Benedetto before going solo in 1981.

"I was working with classical guitar builder Augustine LoPrinzi when Bob came in one day and asked if I would be interested in apprenticing with him to learn to make archtops. I knew this was an opportunity not to be missed, and took him up on it. I ended up working for two years in Bob's shop and probably had a hand in building about fifty of his guitars.

John Buscarino

"When Bob decided to make violins, I bought some tools, took over his Florida shop, and began making guitars on my own. At first I built electric solid-body guitars, then electric acoustics—about 500 in all— before I branched out into archtops and carved-back classicals in 1993.

"My first instruments were pretty much replicas of Bob's guitars. Although his influence will always be there, I think I've developed my own individual style, or whatever it is that makes a Buscarino a Buscarino."

In 1968, Buscarino, who was eighteen, started studying classical guitar. Within a few years, he was playing professionally and working in a music store to make ends meet. Doing repair work on other people's guitars convinced him that he'd rather make instruments than play them.

"I supplemented my income with playing for many years, until the business started to hold its own. Then, as I got busier, I just didn't have the time to do both. I think having played in so many bands over the years contributed to my guitar building. It's nice to have a great-looking guitar, but it's even better to have a great-looking guitar that plays and feels great, too."

Buscarino currently makes three types of guitar: archtop, carved-back classical, and carved-back flat-top steel string. *"I think making all kinds of different guitars really helps with techniques and with coming up with new and innovative ideas that appeal to all sorts of players."*

When asked to become part of the Blue Guitar Project, he didn't hesitate. *"I think that choosing the color blue helped to break down some of the traditional archtop stereotyping. In building the guitar, I learned a lot about what kind of wonderful touches you can add to an archtop to make it a truly beautiful instrument."*

The Buscarino Virtuoso features maple-wood binding with natural-wood purfling of black and blue dyed veneers on the body, headstock, fingerboard, and pickguard. There is a custom tree-of-life inlay on the fingerboard made of abalone and mother-of-pearl, accented with

red coral and blue turquoise. The headstock ornament is mother-of-pearl with turquoise accents, and features ebony tuners with diamond-shaped inlays of blue turquoise. The tailpiece features a scroll with Scott Chinery's signature engraved on it.

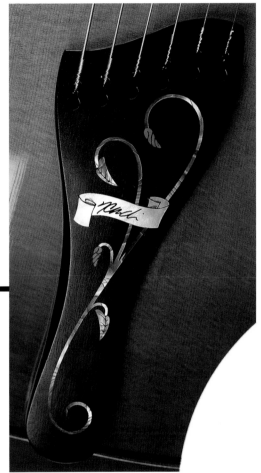

"I believe acoustic archtops represent the epitome of lutherie. You can stand back when it's done in awe of its sheer beauty. It gives you a real sense of accomplishment when you see the finished product.

I don't think I'll ever get out of guitar making. It's in my blood. I'll keep carving until the day I die."

3

"It can be mellow, soft, and sweet, but you can coax it into that roaring, classic archtop sound." Scott Chinery

1995—SERIAL # 720995

CAMPELLONE SPECIAL

Mark Campellone

L ike many of his fellow luthiers, Mark Campellone worked as a professional musician prior to making guitars. He began playing the guitar at age ten. After high school, he completed two semesters of advanced studies at the Berklee College of Music before starting full-time work with various rock and jazz groups. During the mid-1970s, he began *"tinkering with instruments, doing some refinishing experiments and taking apart old guitars."*

Many of the guitars Mark "tinkered" with were Gibson archtops.

"Probably the strongest influence on my work has been the Gibson Guitar Company. My first good guitar was a Gibson, and I've loved them ever since—particularly the styling of their top archtop models. I've done major repair and restoration work on a number of older

Mark Campellone

Gibson archtops, and I found that taking these instruments apart and reassembling them was a great education."

After building a number of solid-body electric bass guitars, Campellone was thirty-three when he made his first archtop in 1988.

"It turned out pretty well and, in terms of timing, coincided with my loss of interest in playing. After my second archtop in 1989, I knew that this was what I wanted to do. I continued doing repair work until 1993, when the demand for my instruments was strong enough for me to become a

Mark Campellone

full-time maker. When I first started building archtops, each instrument took roughly 120 hours. I still work alone at the shop, but now my operation is more streamlined and efficient, allowing me to build twelve guitars every ten weeks. My Blue Guitar was part of a regular production run, but it did include a few special features.

"The most unusual is the paua-shell pickguard, which I chose because of the beauty of its pattern and its varied shades of blue, which complement the color of the guitar. Another special, though subtle, feature is the use of Macassar ebony for the tailpiece applique and bridge.

"The D'Aquisto Blue guitar utilized Macassar ebony for its pickguard and truss-rod cover, and I thought this tie-in would be a nice touch.

"I'm optimistic about the level of interest being shown in archtop guitars. Basically, I feel they're like classic cars—despite all of the modern styling seen on cars today, a classic design like a Rolls Royce still looks great. The archtop fits into our musical culture in the same way. It's a classic instrument associated with a classic musical style, jazz."

"The archtop has always been very attractive to guitar players because it looks good. It has a beautiful appearance. I've noticed over the years that a lot of pop stars have posed with them on their album covers, but they probably haven't used them on the recording because they haven't been practical for their purposes. A lot of older archtops, while they are really great for jazz playing, have not been very adaptable to other forms of music. Now we're seeing these new archtops that are more user friendly."

Martin Taylor

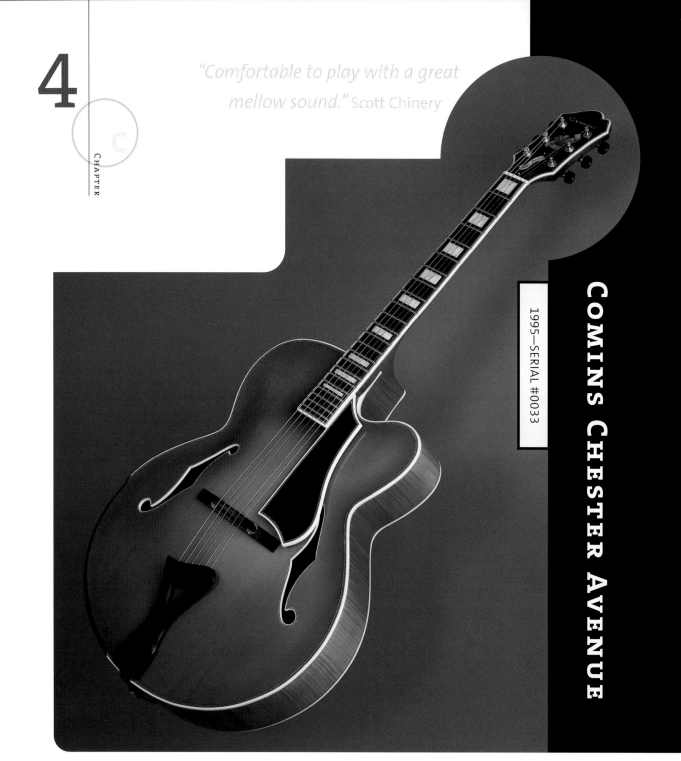

4

"Comfortable to play with a great mellow sound." Scott Chinery

1995—SERIAL #0033

COMINS CHESTER AVENUE

BILL COMINS

B *ill likes to say he's one of the new kids on the block, and that was one of the things that attracted me to his work— a chance to see what the younger luthiers were doing."*

Bill Comins may, as Scott Chinery recounts, be one of the newcomers at age thirty-two, but he's been playing the guitar since he was six years old.

"I majored in jazz guitar performance at Temple University, and that's when I started to dabble in lutherie. After college, while I was teaching and playing local gigs, I started doing repair work for music stores. That evolved into a part-time business. Then, around the time I got married, I went to work full time in a violin shop. I was there for four or five years, pretty much as their main repairman. I learned a lot about the construction of the violin, and how it relates to the guitar."

Like a number of young luthiers, Comins found himself learning the tricks of the trade from Bob Benedetto.

"Bob lived a couple of hours away from me, so I called him and struck up a friendship. He was incredibly helpful in my getting started. I couldn't ask for a better mentor. Another mentor of mine has always been Jimmy D'Aquisto. I never actually met him—just talked to him

on the phone once—but I read every article about him and the way he built his instruments. So I guess he was my earliest influence before I met Bob.

"Once I'd started building my own guitars it was also very helpful to go over to Scott Chinery's and play some of the old D'Angelicos, D'Aquistos, Gibsons, Strombergs, and others. You can really get a feel for what the makers were all about when you can play a number of their instruments at one sitting.

Bill Comins

"I built my first archtop with Benedetto in 1991 and then started buying tools and setting up to make my own line of archtops. It was in 1993 or 1994 that I became a full-time guitar maker. I've made

somewhere over fifty instruments to date. Although I've dabbled in flat-tops and solid bodies, archtops are what I like to do and what I do best.

"I work by myself, and it takes me between 100 and 200 hours to make an archtop. The Blue Guitar took a little longer. The arm and chest chamfers, for instance, make for a more comfortable feeling guitar, but they're very time consuming to execute.

"The burl on the face of the peghead and pickguard is dyed black, and the edges are shaded to give it a more antique look. Getting the blue color was kind of tricky. I had a lot of trouble getting it right where I wanted it.

"Most of my archtops have been fairly traditional in terms of their overall appearance and voice. My guitars are what most jazz players probably expect an archtop to be. While I've done some experimentation, I thought with the Blue I'd just do what I do best.

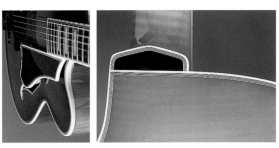

"I think the resurgence in archtops over the past few years has a lot to do with the fact that jazz has become a stable part of popular culture; become legitimized, if you will. There is no sign of violins going out of style, and I believe the same is true of archtops. They are definitely here to stay."

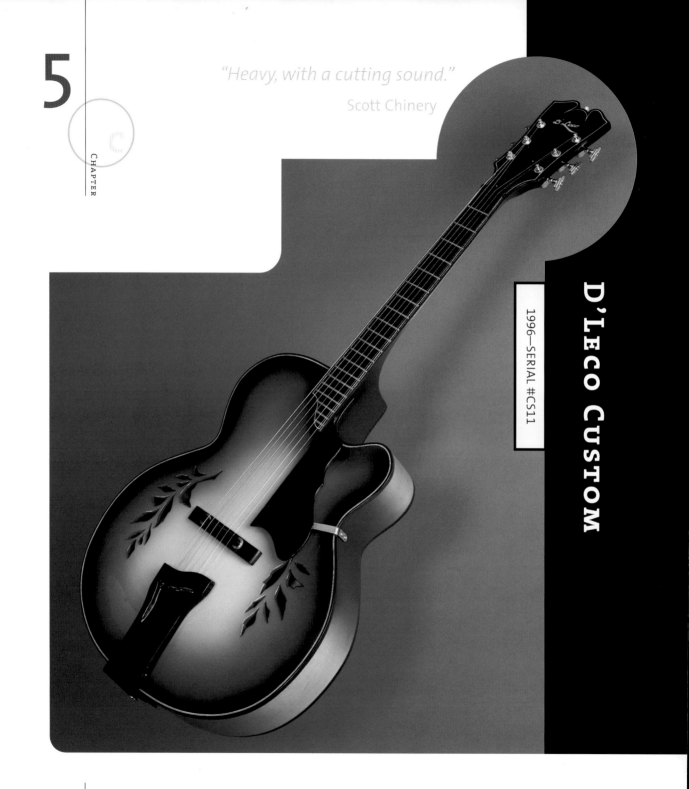

5

CHAPTER

"Heavy, with a cutting sound."

Scott Chinery

1996—SERIAL #CS11

D'LECO CUSTOM

D'Leco Guitars

D'Leco Guitars in Oklahoma City is a partnership of two guitar enthusiasts, James Dale and Maurice Johnson. Jim, whose father fronted a western swing band back in the early 1940s, is the luthier, while Maurice, a graphic artist and fellow player, handles the marketing.

"I got my first guitar at about age eight," recalls Jim, *"and began admiring the way that instruments were made, particularly the L-5s and Super 400s played by my father's sidemen.*

"My early influences were masters such as John D'Angelico, Lloyd Loar, and Elmer Stromberg. I guess I gathered up every picture of a guitar I could find, mostly things available at the local music store. Back then, the clamor in the guitar industry wasn't very big. Nothing like today."

In 1953, Jim made two solid bodies as a high school project. After the death of his father forty years later, Jim, then a cabinetmaker, decided to fulfill a dream he'd shared with his dad to build quality guitars.

D'Leco Guitars

"*I guess that traditional would best describe my approach. I especially like the old instruments. They were very solid. Nothing sounded better in the rhythm section than an old unamplified guitar laying down a beat that just made the horn section swing. Like Freddie Green, with the Basie Band, for example. Of course, a solo instrument in these surroundings required amplification.*"

The D'Leco partnership acquired rights to the name of legendary jazz guitarist Charlie Christian and produced a special "tribute" model in his honor. It was the publicity surrounding this guitar that put D'Leco in the frame to build one of the Blue Guitars.

"*I guess that traditional would best describe my approach. I especially like the old instruments. They were very solid.*"

"It was," Jim says, "quite a surprise and a pleasant treat to be invited. I'm now fifty-seven years old and probably one of the oldest luthiers out there. I plan to continue building guitars at our present pace for at least another five or six years. After that, an occasional instrument will be enough to keep in practice and keep the fire of love for the instrument glowing."

According to Chinery, D'Leco's approach to the Blue was different than the other luthiers.

"Jim made a much heavier, thicker guitar that created a more cutting sound than the more open instruments. Visually it's a stunner. I especially like the way the soundholes are created with a botanical motif. I suspect it would work best amplified, although when it comes to amplified acoustics, I'm a bit of a purist. For me, to put a pickup on one of these guitars would be like painting flames on the side of a Ferrari."

6

CHAPTER

"A cheeky sound—very dynamic, bell-like." Steve Howe

1996—SERIAL #01

FENDER D'AQUISTO CUSTOM ULTRA

FENDER CUSTOM SHOP

The Fender D'Aquisto Custom Ultra is not simply a D'Aquisto-style guitar named in his honor. It is, or would be if such things existed, a "virtual" D'Aquisto.

D'Aquisto had worked with the Fender Corporation on various projects for about fifteen years before his death. Having manufactured a D'Aquisto line in Japan for a number of years, in 1993 Fender decided to move the project to its custom shop in California. Stephen Stern, who had recently joined the company, was selected to head up the venture.

"When John Page, general manager of the custom shop, offered me the job, which meant the chance to work with the master himself, James D'Aquisto, I didn't hesitate."

Stern, who is forty, comes to lutherie from the world of cabinetmaking.

"My first interest in building musical instruments came when I was ninteen.

Stephen Stern

Stephen Stern

I wanted to join a rock band, so I bought my first electric guitar, a Fender Stratocaster.

"I wasn't very successful as a player, but I still very much wanted to be in the music business in some capacity.

"Having worked on custom office furniture for more than five years after high school, my woodworking skills were a lot better than my guitar playing ability. I got a job at Charvel Guitars, where I stayed for four years, getting a good education in instrument making while doing repair work on my own time. Then I heard about the opening at Fender, and here I am.

"I would say without a doubt that working with Jimmy D'Aquisto was the greatest experience of my career. Jimmy taught me how the archtop guitar works in a way that I could visualize; not in abstract theory but in plain, simple English."

D'Aquisto died in California while consulting for Fender. According to Scott Chinery, the D'Aquisto Custom Ultra is as much Jimmy's as it is Stern's.

"As soon as you pick it up and play it you know it must be a D'Aquisto. Stern was very successful in translating what was one of D'Aquisto's last designs."

"I've always been inspired by the instruments of the '40s, '50s and '60s," says Stern.

"I love the designs of the old Gibsons, D'Angelicos, and D'Aquistos.

"The standards I set for my guitars are smooth arches, tight joints, a comfortable neck, great playability, and, of course, beautiful tone. I've made approximately eighty guitars since making my first in 1981, including some solid bodies, but now I strictly make archtops."

In addition to having become a premiere contemporary archtop maker, Stern also has realized his other dream; he plays in a classic rock band that gigs around the Pasadena area.

"Has that familiar, edgy, Gibson sound." Steve Howe

1996

GIBSON SUPER 400 CUSTOM

GIBSON CUSTOM SHOP

I n the years since Orville Gibson carved that first archtop, the Gibson Company has produced a number of historically significant instruments, two of the most important being the 1923 L-5 and 1934 Super 400 archtop guitars. The Blue Guitar Project gave the luthiers in Gibson's custom shop the chance to make what Scott Chinery refers to as *"the super Super 400."*

Unlike the other Blue Guitars, which were built by individual makers, the Blue Super 400 was created by a team of specialized luthiers whose combined experience building Gibson guitars totaled more than 160 years.

Gibson Guitars

The team was led by the senior design engineer of Gibson's Historic Collection, Jim "Hutch" Hutchins, whose thirty-three years on the job have made him the company's longest-tenured employee.

The rest of the Super 400 team, along with their areas of responsibility, were Dick Ickes, rough top carving and layup of back and top; Phil Ashworth, top graduation and layout of bracing; Felix Wallace, binding of the *f*-holes; Butch Wallace, rabbeting and body binding; Todd Harrison, fleur-de-lis inlay; Gary Winsett, fingerboard binding; Kareem Haddad, final assembly; Mickey McGuire, spraying; Wanda Johnson, binding scraping; and Tim Evans, buffing. The fingerboard and peghead inlays were done by Rockford Carving.

The Super 400 was a fancy, high-end guitar when it debuted in 1934, and it still is. The custom shop team added a few special touches to make the Blue Super 400 stand alone. Abalone was substituted for mother-of-pearl in all the diagonal bar inlays on the fingerboard and peghead. Rosewood inserts were added to the tailpiece, and abalone fleurs-de-lis were inlaid into the pickguard as well as into one of the tailpiece inserts.

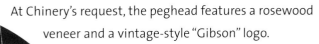

At Chinery's request, the peghead features a rosewood veneer and a vintage-style "Gibson" logo. His initials, SRC, were added to the heelcap.

What does Chinery, who has the world's largest collection of Super 400s, think of the end result?

"When I first got this guitar, I was a little skeptical since I've already played all of the greatest Super 400s in existence. But, without question, this is the best-sounding Super 400 I have ever played."

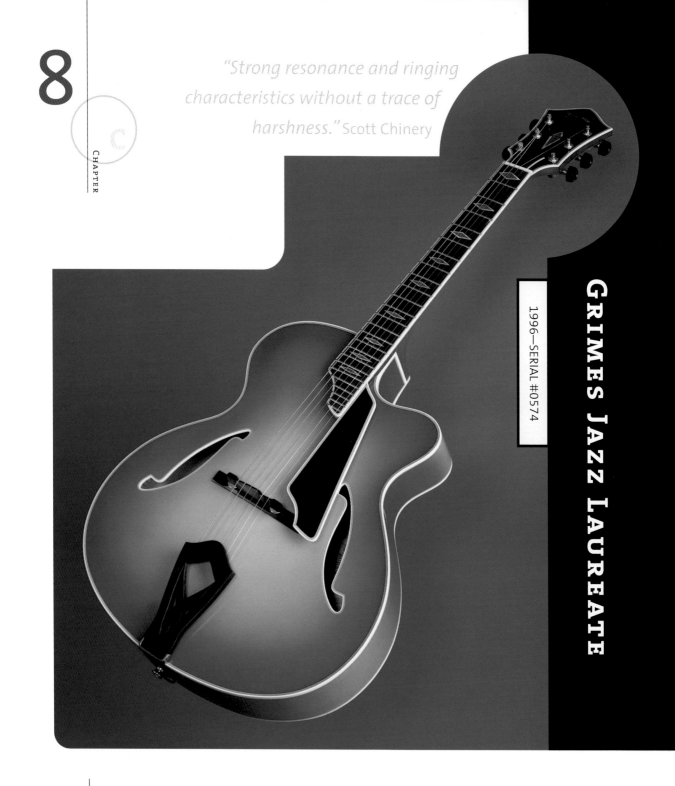

8

"Strong resonance and ringing characteristics without a trace of harshness." Scott Chinery

1996—SERIAL #0574

GRIMES JAZZ LAUREATE

STEVE GRIMES

Steve Grimes

Steve Grimes was born in 1948 into what, in retrospect, would seem to be the perfect family for a future luthier. His father was a carpenter, and his mother played the violin.

It was while playing in a rock band in the mid-sixties that Grimes first became interested in working on musical instruments.

"I successfully dismantled and reassembled my electric guitar, for no particular reason; but I was impressed that it worked afterward. I started dabbling in guitar repair not long after that."

Grimes continued doing part-time repair work while employed as a full-time draftsman at Boeing, but he finally realized that he had to choose one job or the other.

"I was very bored with my job at Boeing, and although I hadn't yet established lutherie as a profitable venture, I quit Boeing and set up a small shop for building archtop mandolins and doing instrument repairs. I built my first mandolin in 1972, and my first archtop guitar in 1974.

"I was also working two or three nights a week in various bands, playing everything from bluegrass to old swing jazz.

"My commitment to making instruments full time was not a painstaking decision. It was more like the craft made the decision for me. It consumed me. But it wasn't until about 1980 that I started seeing the light at the end of the tunnel financially."

A self-professed traditionalist, Grimes was a bit taken aback by the thought of making a bright blue guitar.

"I believe Jimmy D'Aquisto has been the most influential force in the evolution of the archtop guitar, and his ideas have strongly influenced my guitar designs, up to a point.

"While I liked some of the not-so-subtle nuances in design, such as streamlined f-holes and 'open' pegheads, I hadn't yet accepted wildly colored finishes. I guess I had the feeling that any colors on an archtop should be wood-related hues. The Blue Guitar Project gave me the opportunity to break out of the mold and try something new.

"My Blue Guitar probably took about two hundred hours to build. It features a European spruce top, European maple sides and back, and ebony fingerboard, bridge, pickguard, tailpiece, and peghead overlay. The inlay in the peghead is a double diamond of lapis, surrounded by mother-of-pearl.

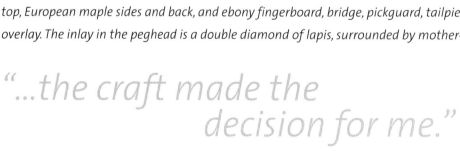
"...the craft made the decision for me."

"I liked the fact that although there were a few criteria predetermined by Chinery, the overall design was left up to the maker, with no limits or restrictions. We were, in fact, encouraged to outdo ourselves and create something totally unique."

For Chinery, the sound produced by the Grimes guitar was quite a suprise.

"The finished instrument is as far away from the traditional archtop in terms of sound as anything I've ever heard. It's very open. It has a quality that goes even beyond a flat-top with its strong resonance and ringing characteristics."

Grimes is also conscious of the ways in which the archtop is expanding into what used to be flat-top territory.

"I believe that a lot of flat-top players are becoming aware of what the archtop can do that their flat-tops, or classic guitars, can't; and they are opening up to that kind of sound.

"I also think the popularity of the archtop parallels an increased interest in jazz styles among previously exclusive rock, blues, and new acoustic-style players." To date Grimes has made 526 instruments, of which 185 are archtop guitars.

"I'll tell you, even after twenty-five years, I still can't wait to get into the shop every morning. The feeling of satisfaction I get from hearing one of my instruments in the hands of a really gifted player makes all of the hard work worthwhile—and then some."

Steve Grimes with jazz great George Benson

9

"A classic archtop sound. It has a sort of glassy depth to it that is quite nice."

Steve Howe

1996—SERIAL #76

HOLLENBECK EBONY 'N' BLUE

BILL HOLLENBECK

ill Hollenbeck grew up in central Illinois in a family that could have hired out as a small combo featuring piano, organ, saxophone, and guitar.

During his high school and college years, Bill did minor repair work on guitars. A high school electronics teacher for twenty-five years, he retired in 1990 to devote himself to full-time guitar building, restoration, and repair.

Bill Hollenbeck

"About three years after I'd started my teaching career I met Bill Barker, a well-known midwest luthier with a good following in that part of the country. After about an hour spent talking with him, I knew that I wanted to make archtop guitars. I worked as his apprentice, mostly on weekends and summer vacations, for about twenty years assisting in the building of numerous guitars. I helped to build about 50 of the 115 guitars he made before he passed away.

Bill Hollenbeck

"I built my first guitar in 1975, and I've constructed almost 80 to date, all archtops. Needless to say, there's a lot of Barker in the guitars I build today."

Among players, Hollenbeck's guitars are known for their mid-range acoustic attack. This, according to Bill, is because he designs them around the harp and piano. *"The mothers of all stringed instruments,"* as he puts it.

"I used an extremely dense bird's-eye sugar maple for the back, sides, and neck; gold Schaller machine heads with ebony buttons; a five-piece neck with two contrasting strips running its length; and ebony for the fingerboard, truss-rod cover, bridge, saddle, and pick-guard, as well as the trim on the gold tail piece.

"Somewhere on all of my guitars I always inlay a fleur-de-lis. On the Ebony 'n' Blue, I cut an ebony inlay and mounted it on the back, close to the neck."

As many of his compatriots were, Hollenbeck was somewhat surprised to be asked to build a blue archtop.

"In my twenty-six years of building archtops, I had never seen a blue one. But they told me that one of Jimmy D'Aqusito's last guitars was blue, so blue it would be."

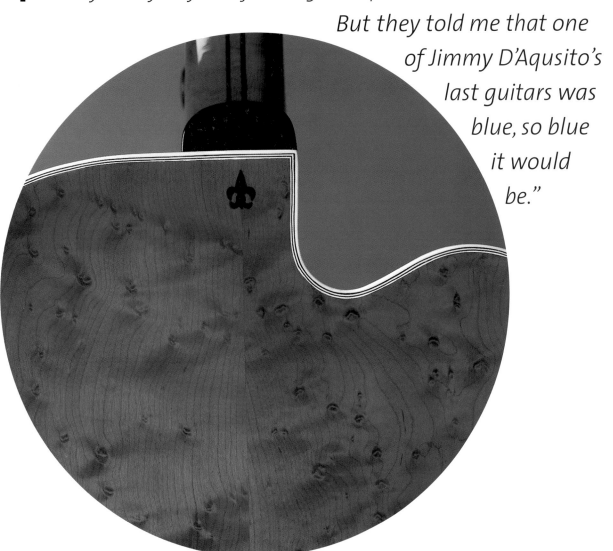

"It has stinging trebles. The kind that make me concerned for my wife's good china if I play it in the house." Scott Chinery

1996—SERIAL #0040

LACEY VIRTUOSO

MARK LACEY

Australian by birth, Mark Lacey nonetheless spent almost all of his first twenty-four years in London, where he lived until 1977.

"I got my first guitar when I was five years old. It was a six-string flat-top, Italian, I think. I always remember doing adjustments and string changes myself, since there wasn't anyone to ask for advice about it."

During his time in England, Mark went to school, apprenticed in mechanical engineering with the Glacier Bearing Company, played in a band called Chancery Lane, and studied musical instrument technology at the London College of Furniture & Interior Design.

"I spent the first two years at college building mostly early fretted instruments from the Renaissance and Baroque periods. These included lutes, citerns, viols, and guitars. They were challenging to build and helped me develop a good feel for intricate decoration. During my third and final year, I concentrated on building modern fretted guitars.

"In 1977 I moved to Oslo, Norway, where I spent the next four years working as a repairman for Norway's largest importer of musical instruments, Norsk Musikk Instrument Co. During this time, I also attended repair courses at the Ovation, Peavey, and Hohner factories."

In 1981, well-known vintage guitar expert and dealer George Gruhn helped Lacey emigrate to America, where he began to study older American archtop and flat-top guitars.

The next seven years saw Lacey working in various capacities, such as running a guitar shop and doing guitar repairs. He also did a nine-month stint as quality control and design engineer for Guild Guitars in Rhode Island.

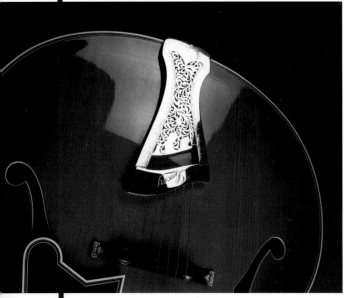

"Having been laid off from Guild, I decided to return to Los Angeles and start my own custom guitar shop. In July 1988, I opened the Guitar Garage just off the Sunset Strip.

"In 1995, my wife and I moved to Nashville, where I have set up a workshop. I have been concentrating on making archtop and semi-solid-body electric guitars, and I plan to expand my line to include a few flat-tops.

"My main influences have been John D'Angelico, Jimmy D'Aquisto, and Gibson. I have tried to stay fairly traditional in my designs, which I believe is what most players want. Having done a great deal of repair work over the years, one learns how not to build a guitar.

"My main objective, besides building guitars that sound good, is to build guitars that will last. The goal is to find the perfect balance between sound and strength. D'Angelico, D'Aquisto, and Stromberg knew this, and that's what makes their guitars so great."

Lacey and Chinery had known about each other for some time before the Blue Guitar Project.

"Several years ago, on the advice of a vintage guitar dealer, Scott had planned to come out to Los Angeles to see the first Virtuoso I'd made. He cancelled the trip due to a cold, which was a good thing because a major earthquake hit the day he was due to visit.

"My own Blue Guitar took around four months to build. Some of its notable features include the tailpiece, which is made of brass, has a soap-pierced design cut into it, and is engraved and plated in 18-carat gold.

"The bound ebony pickguard is inlaid and engraved with a mother-of-pearl butterfly and the mother-of-pearl neck inlays are intricately hand engraved. There are also pearl inlays at the ends of the bridge.

"I was interested in the design innovations incorporated into some of the Blue Guitars. I feel that moving the soundholes away from the bridge results in a louder instrument with improved bass response. Also, I liked the idea of adding an extra soundhole at the upper bout. I may build something along these lines, as I feel the archtop will probably evolve in this direction."

"The archtop is still developing. One of the things that Scott Chinery did with the Blue Guitars was to plant some ideas in the minds of the makers, like having adjustable soundhole openings placed in the side of the guitar so the player can hear the sound better. As a result of this, there are a few quite revolutionary guitars in the collection. These are the sort of ideas that can lead to other things. Nothing should really stand still, it should keep moving."
Martin Taylor

"An angry, gypsy sound. It has a soul about it that's very interesting." Steve Howe

BOZO CHICAGOAN

1996—SERIAL #501-4

Bozo Podunavac

As a kid," Scott Chinery recalls, "I bought a Leo Kottke album. One of the songs was played on a 12-string, and I remember being dazzled by the tone of the guitar. I did some research and found out he was playing a Bozo."

Bozo Podunavac, who emigrated to Chicago in 1959 from Belgrade, Yugoslavia, grew up in decidedly unmusical circumstances.

"I was born in 1928. When World War II broke out, we were expelled from our home, and I spent the war years herding sheep and hiding from the Nazis. When we returned home in 1945, everything was either destroyed or missing.

"I worked for a while as a toolmaker, but was arrested for discussing politics and ended up spending eleven months as a prisoner, doing hard labor building aqueducts for hydro-electric power plants. After I was released, I moved to Beograd, where I was introduced to woodworking and discovered a love for making musical instruments which has never left me."

Bozo Podunavac

Bozo studied for five years with the leading Yugoslavian luthier, Milutin Madenovic. After passing the mandatory government examinations, he was licensed to open his own business, doing instrument repair and making 5-string tamburitzas.

"Beginning about 1950, I started to do repair work on many varied types of instruments. The first guitar which bore my name was made in the kitchen of my house in 1960. To date, my records show about 450 guitars. I am unsure of the exact number, because I did not number the early ones."

Once settled in Chicago, Bozo began doing repair work for various dealers and for the Chicago Symphony Orchestra.

"After becoming well known as a maker of flat-top guitars, I decided in 1975 or 1976 to try my first archtop, but I continued to specialize in the flat-tops. It is only recently, in the past two years, that I have begun making 'jazz' guitars again. I am constantly looking for new designs, but I use traditional materials because wood gives the best resonance and overall sound."

One of the unique features to be found on the Bozo Chicagoan is the elaborate inlay work, done with a combination of abalone and pearl and then overlaid with a blue finish. The signature oversize headstock, pickguard, and tailpiece are further examples of Bozo's detailed craftsmanship.

As a companion piece to the Chicagoan, Podunavac built a Baby Blue Bozo that, according to Chinery, is *"a masterpiece in its own right. It has a sound that will cut through a six-foot lead wall. Bozo has recognized that there are many new tonal possibilities with the archtop, and he's exploring them all."*

When asked to explain the secret to getting such a big sound from such a small instrument, Bozo told all.

"My Baby Blue version of the Chicagoan is a half-scale version of the original. The strings are made of Kryptonite, which was given to me by Superman. That is what gives the instrument the power to penetrate lead walls."

"Sounds like one of the great D'Angelico New Yorkers." Scott Chinery

1996—SERIAL #04960218

TRIGGS NEW YORKER

JIM TRIGGS

I attempted my first instrument, a mandolin, in 1975. I was about nineteen and had gotten into bluegrass music in high school, and learned to play guitar, banjo, and mandolin. I bought a how-to book, got out my father's woodworking tools, and built the thing in my parents' driveway. I used an electric drill with a rasp bit to do the top and back, and I just burned up that drill."

Jim Triggs, who has been described as the "P. T. Barnum" of guitar makers, worked at a number of odd jobs as he taught himself to build mandolins and violins, first in Kansas, where he grew up, and then in California.

"I'm a self-taught instrument builder, but I was definitely influenced by John D'Angelico, Elmer Stromberg, and Lloyd Loar. The first guitars I built in the early 1980s were all flat-tops. Up until I went to work for Gibson in 1986, I had built around 125 instruments, mostly mandolins and mandolas, as well as a couple of banjos and flat-tops."

During the time Triggs worked for Gibson in Nashville, he got to study the work of one of his influences first-hand and, better yet, to work with another of them.

"I worked at Gibson from 1988 to 1992. While there, I studied Lloyd Loar's design of archtop instruments, mostly mandolins. The way I build my guitars on the inside reflects my study of Lloyd's ideas. When I build one, it's really just a big mandolin to me. I think that's what Lloyd and the other archtop makers who started out building mandolins were achieving. That approach forces you to be really accurate.

"Jimmy D'Aquisto, who was soon to become associated with Gibson, became a good friend during the last few years of his life. He designed my current "J.Triggs" logo that appears on the peghead of all my guitars. I would say that I haven't really taken any of Jimmy's design ideas, but I admired his passion for guitar building, and for life in general. I think my passion for making guitars is evident in each and every one. I look at each instrument as a piece of fine art, as Jimmy did with his instruments."

As the head design engineer for Gibson, Triggs was in charge of the archtop line and was responsible for the construction of about five hundred archtops, as well as fifty or more other instruments.

When he left Gibson in 1992, Triggs began making replicas of D'Angelico guitars; but at the urging of D'Aquisto and others, he soon began making instruments under his own name.

Triggs's Blue Guitar is a good example of what *20th Century Guitar* magazine referred to as his *"more is more"* philosophy.

"It has D-45 Martin-style abalone trim around the top, f-holes, neck, peghead, and back. Underneath, the ivoroid binding is white-and-blue check marquetry. There's also a solid abalone pickguard and probably the first sunburst fingerboard in the history of guitar building. The tailpiece is highly engraved in a scroll and gun pattern.

"I thought the project was a cool idea, and I tried to build the best instrument of my career." Triggs is working on a number of new archtop design projects that will

"be as different from a D'Angelico as a Steinberger is from a '59 Les Paul."

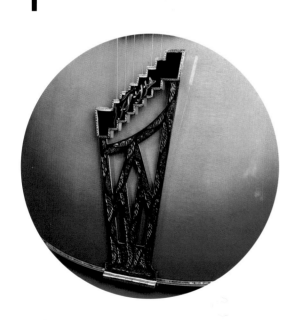

"BLUE TOMORROWS" by Leslie Jean-Bart

THE MODERNISTS

A tune beyond us as we are,
Yet nothing changed by the blue guitar;
Ourselves in the tune as if in space,
Yet nothing changed, except the place
Of things as they are and only the place
As you play them, on the blue guitar,
Placed, so, beyond the compass of change,
Perceived in a final atmosphere;
For a moment final, in the way
The thinking of art seems final when
The thinking of god is smoky dew.
The tune is space. The blue guitar
Becomes the place of things as they are,
A composing of senses of the guitar.

Excerpt from "Man with the Blue Guitar," by Wallace Stevens

"A sound almost as big as Texas."

Scott Chinery

1996

COLLINGS CUSTOM

BILL COLLINGS

Bill Collings

*B*ill Collings was born August 9, 1948 in Midland, Michigan, and was raised in Ohio. He started playing a C-1 Gibson at the age of thirteen (after all, Elvis was King). He attended Ohio University where, without any formal training, he built banjo parts. A combination of reckless-ness, a love for motorcycles, and a lack of interest in medical school led him to Texas in the mid-seventies. A lifelong interest in guitars, tools, and machinery challenged him to attempt some stringed-instrument building and repair. His lack of direction got him where he is today."*

That's how Bill Collings tells it, and he should know. From a single guitar in 1973, Collings Guitars now has nineteen full-time employees and shipped about 750 guitars in 1996, all but a few of them flat-tops. Collings, unlike most of the luthiers profiled here, is primarily a flat-top maker, finding time for a few archtops whenever he can.

"The last few years I've had time for about four per year. For several years now, I have been fighting to make more, with the thought of introducing them into my production schedule.

"But I've decided I would rather make fewer and make them really nice. What I would like to see in the near future would be ten to fifteen archtops per year. You can reshape the voice of an archtop from the more traditional style to get more sustain, more roundness in the treble, clean, clear bass, and balance like a flat-top. But the archtop is fundamentally a different guitar, the sound comes off of it rather than out of it like a flat-top. I think this difference should be enhanced."

Another way in which Collings stands apart from many of his contemporaries is in his use of computers and other state-of-the-art manufacturing techniques. His guitar assembly room has a $45,000 climate-control system that maintains a constant temperature of seventy-two degrees and 48 percent humidity to prevent his woods from shrinking, warping, and cracking.

"It's expensive, but without it we couldn't do anything. Guitars have to be made in the right environment."

"Guitars have to be made in the right environment."

He also has a CAD/CAM (computer-aided design and manufacture) Fadal Vertical Machining Center for the accurate machining of many parts like necks, bridges, and fret boards for his production guitars.

All of this technology is utilized, he says, for one purpose only: to make the best possible guitar.

"With every instrument I make, I'm searching for that special sound that only the finest instruments have. Every guitar must be a special guitar. As for the Blue Guitars, I thought the idea was kind of weird. Then I realized that to commemorate Jimmy's work and to show the world his influence in all of our guitars would be wonderful."

Among the outstanding features of the Blue Custom, described by its maker as, *"an eighteen-inch with whitewalls,"* are the broken-glass fragments inlaid in the neck and headstock and the intensity of the blue finish, which manages to stand out even in such illustrious company.

"A flat-top, certainly a steel-string, has more of a sustain to it, more of a singing sound, while the archtop usually has a slightly closed-in sound, the notes don't ring in the same way."
Martin Taylor

"Great for classical music and you can also make it howl." Scott Chinery

1996—SERIAL #1042

MANZER BLUE ABSYNTHE

Linda Manzer

Canadian Linda Manzer "made" her first guitar at age twelve. Under the spell of Beatlemania she sawed an acoustic guitar in half to make it *"look like George Harrison's guitar."* Her hopes of studying woodworking at school during this period were dashed when she was forced to study home economics, where young ladies were expected to make tea and biscuits for the boys.

The Nova Scotia College of Art and Design in Halifax had a less provincial attitude, allowing Manzer's woodworking skills to flourish as she became expert in the making of folk instruments such as dulcimers.

While still a student, she made a fateful visit to the studio of a Canadian luthier named Jean Larrivee.

"I'll never forget that day. The room had all the warm color of the dust in the lamplight, and this young guy was sitting on an old stool sanding a carved peghead. As soon as I walked in I thought, 'This is it, I want to do this. I want to be sitting on that stool.'"

She wanted it badly enough to quit art school and become one of Larrivee's apprentices. Manzer remained with him for three and

Gerald Allain

a half years, learning all aspects of flat-top guitar construction before setting up her own guitar-making shop in 1978.

Another career milestone came in 1982, when she met Pat Metheny backstage after a concert. When she handed him one of her guitars, he couldn't put it down.

"He ended up playing the whole concert over again on my guitar."

That first encounter led to an association that has resulted in Manzer building sixteen guitars for Metheny, including one with four necks, two soundholes, and forty-two strings called the Pikasso.

"In addition to making both archtop and flat-top guitars, I have designed and built a number of unusual instruments including the Pikasso, the sitarguitar, the harp/sitarguitar, the baritone guitar, the little Manzer, and a charango. Not counting the one I butchered at age twelve, my first real guitar was a flat-top completed in 1975. Since then, I've made approximately three hundred instruments."

Not long after that backstage encounter, Manzer received a grant to study archtop building with Jimmy D'Aquisto at his Long Island studio. For her, participating in the Blue Guitar Project brought back memories of those days in D'Aquisto's workshop.

"I began making archtops in Jimmy's studio, so his death affected me greatly. While the Blue Absynthe may not be an actual 'tribute' guitar, there is no question that his memory had a big influence on my own interpretation of the Blue Guitar."

It normally takes about two hundred hours to complete one of her archtops. The Blue Absynthe, with its special features, took five months.

"As soon as I accepted the commission, I selected several sets of woods and began visualizing the guitar. I have a policy of not beginning a project until I have a very clear idea of the final instrument in my mind.

"It's named after absinthe, a liqueur that was very popular in turn-of-the-century France. Highly intoxicating, it was the favorite of many artists because it inspired visions and creativity. It eventually was outlawed because, done to excess, it could also cause insanity and, sometimes, death. I chose the name because, like the 18-inch archtop, it's an intoxicating, mythical elixir.

"The wood is European spruce and European maple. The fingerboard, tailpiece, pickguard, and bridge are all ebony, as are all the bindings. I was trying for an elegant look, with all wood appointments, and not too flashy. I figured that, with the sliding panel door and the blue color, it was best to keep the other detailing rather simple." Manzer was one of the luthiers Chinery asked to design a side soundhole. "I always enjoy a challenge and decided to make a sliding door panel so the size of the hole could be changed, depending on how much of the sound the player wanted redirected.

"The door is made of two thin veneers of wood, ebony and curly maple. It's very thin but stiff, and glued in a compound curve to move smoothly along mahogany tracks inside the guitar. In the open position, it could be compared to a flat-top sound. Closed, it projects like a traditional archtop.

"I'll be honest—I didn't think much of archtops in the early part of my career. I thought they were wonderful looking but sounded chunky. But listening to and playing a D'Aquisto changed that. I realized that there was some real magic that I hadn't seen or heard before that moment. I was hooked."

"A delicate, feminine sort of sound. Well-rounded in its balance. A guitar that responds well to being played gently." Steve Howe

MEGAS CUSTOM

TED MEGAS

Ted Megas was drawn toward music in general and the guitar in particular in the mid-1960s.

"I was interested in the guitar itself as much as the music it produced. While I was in high school in Bethlehem, Pennsylvania, I formed a rock group and because my father had a workshop in the basement, I was able to begin doing modifications to the guitars I owned.

"I attended Ohio State University as an engineering student, but the constraints of college didn't agree with me. I was much more interested in playing jazz fusion guitar and trying to find musicians with the same musical goals."

After relocating to San Francisco in 1973, Megas saw a book on building guitars and realized that that was what he wanted to do.

Ted Megas

"By then I had started to make my living as a furniture- and cabinetmaker. I made my first guitar, a Les Paul–type, carved-top solid body in 1975. Over the next few years, I built ten electric guitars before attempting my first archtop in 1989. I felt that building archtops was a better combination of my interests, knowledge, and skills."

Megas has successfully made the transition to full-time guitar maker, building eight to ten instruments per year. *"I build only archtops, spending an average of two hundred hours on each guitar.*

"The Blue Guitar is the first 18-inch version of my Apollo model. I decided to use cocobolo wood throughout the guitar wherever ebony is normally used, for parts such as the peghead, fingerboard, bridge, and pickguard. Cocobolo was also used for the wood bindings and tuning knobs.

"When it's quartersawn, this wood has a beautiful, multihued, striped appearance. I think it makes an interesting contrast to the blue color.

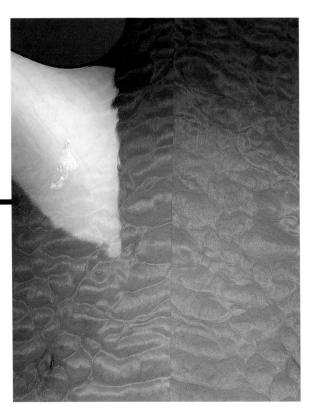

"I appreciate the traditional archtop sound, but the fun, challenge, and reward for me is to experiment. I want to see what the range of the archtop is. I want to design the guitar to get the sound that I'm looking for—the warm, mellow, yet focused sound of the traditional archtop—while moving the guitar in the direction of the fuller and more open sound of the flat-top."

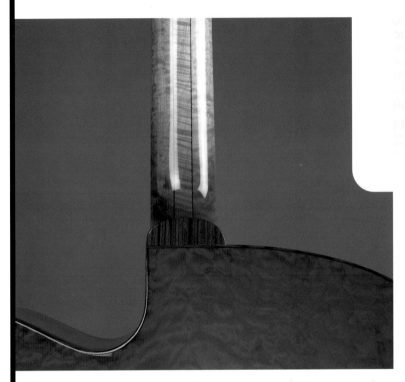

"I appreciate the traditional archtop sound, but the fun, challenge, and reward for me is to experiment."

"When people ask the difference between a flat-top and an archtop, it's a bit like asking the difference between a flute and a clarinet; you blow into both of them, press your fingers over holes, and make sounds. I think the sound of the two guitars is very different, yet closely related, a bit like a violin and a viola. The archtop was an incredible development. The concept of bringing the violin family closer to the guitar allowed the guitar to become part of a different kind of music, whereas the flat-top has never really gotten away from the lute and the early Spanish guitar.

"From a player's point of view, what one plays on a flat-top is developed because of all those past guitars just as much as because people want to play that kind of music. I could country pick on an archtop. I don't, but I could."
Steve Howe

*"Full blooded—very contemporary
—a completely round sound."*

Steve Howe

1995—SERIAL #166

MONTELEONE ROCKET
CONVERTIBLE

JOHN MONTELEONE

 John Monteleone was born in New York in 1947 and grew up in a family for whom playing music was a regular activity.

"My father played the mandolin, and my mother had something of a poor excuse for a guitar as far back as I can remember. I became afflicted with the guitar disease quite early, maybe around six years old. Gene Autry and Roy Rogers helped to get me hooked.

"My first attempt at building a guitar came when I was eleven or twelve. It was a triple-neck steel guitar. For some reason, I lost interest in it and started work on a flat-top dreadnought, which I finally completed about four years later."

While studying for his degree in applied music at Tarkio College in Missouri, Monteleone performed professionally on a number of instruments.

"I played guitar in a folk-style singing duo, as well as valve trombone and string bass in a jazz quartet."

When he returned to Long Island after college, Monteleone found work as a repairman at one of the country's best known vintage fretted-instrument shops, Mandolin Brothers on Staten Island.

John Monteleone

"My experience repairing and restoring a variety of fretted instruments helped a great deal in my work as a luthier, particularly since I've never apprenticed with another maker. I believe that my understanding of what makes a musical instrument bad is equally as valuable as knowing what makes one good.

"Besides archtop guitars, I also make archtop mandolins and flat-top guitars. All together, I've made approximately 260 instruments."

Monteleone's normal production schedule allows between four and eight weeks to complete an archtop guitar. The Blue Guitar, with its two side soundholes and ported front soundhole, was constructed over a period of about six months, during which Monteleone actually made two of them.

"I'd proposed to build a version of my top-of-the-line Radio City model, and I was well along with it when I realized that the side soundhole concept that Scott had asked me to include wouldn't work properly on that guitar.

"I immediately made a new set of guitar sides so that I could experiment with the two side soundholes. I finally settled on a double wall, with the outer guitar side and an inner wall separated by spacers. The resulting sidewall is very rigid and strong. I also carved outer rings of ebony to fit the three soundholes,

"I also make archtop mandolins and flat-top guitars."

John Monteleone

which gave it increased strength and an improved venturi ported surface with smooth edges for a cleaner, unobstructed transference of sound waves.

"All three soundholes have sliding panels that open and close the holes. These were installed for the dual purpose of directing the sound response to either the player or audience, or both at the same time.

"I also decided not to make a pickguard, at least in the traditional sense of the term. Instead, I sculpted a small piece of ebony to form a rest for the fingers. The only ornamention was the ivory inlays, which were recycled from the restoration of my Steinway piano. When it was finally finished, it was really gratifying to be able to demonstrate the effect of each soundhole indivdually by operating the sliding panels."

"I also decided not to make a pickguard, at least in the traditional sense of the term."

"The kind of instrument that makes you sound better than you are."

Scott Chinery

NICKERSON EQUINOX CUSTOM

1996—SERIAL #9496

BRAD NICKERSON

Brad Nickerson

Brad Nickerson, who was born and raised on Cape Cod, showed an early interest in music. Unlike many of his fellow Blue Guitar luthiers, however, no one in his family was involved in either music or craft work.

"I got my first guitar when I was fourteen, but I didn't think about building one until I was nearly forty."

After attending Berklee College of Music, Nickerson worked in the graphic arts field for many years. He maintained his interest in music, playing the guitar professionally on occasion and doing instrument repair work at shops in Boston and Amherst, Massachusetts. Prior to attempting to build his first guitar, Nickerson received advice and encouragement from Cape Cod bow maker and violin luthier, Donald MacKenzie.

"I didn't actually apprentice with anyone, but when I decided to make my first archtop in 1983, both Donald MacKenzie and New York luthier Carlo Greco were a big help.

"I make archtops and flat-tops, as well as full and semihollow-body electrics. To date, I've built about seventy-five instruments, including a solid-body electric dulcimer that I made way back when. My archtops normally take about four weeks to complete, but the Blue Guitar ended up taking me about eight months from start to finish.

"I developed a new model for the project with different placement and shape of the soundholes. I feel that this design, in conjunction with the bracing pattern, both gives the guitar a warmer tone and directs some of the sound toward the player's ear.

"If there's one feature that everyone seems to comment on, it's the wonderful engraving of the blue hyacinth

"If there's one feature that everyone seems to comment on, it's the wonderful engraving of the blue hyacinth macaw."

macaw, done by Petria Mitchell of Brattleboro, Vermont.

"Two primary influences on my guitar making are Orville Gibson and C. F. Martin. Aesthetically, I've been most inspired by Jimmy D'Aquisto's sense of style and his desire to bring the archtop into the twenty-first century.

"Personally, I'd like to see some new things explored on the instrument, taking it in some new directions. A lot of the new acoustic modern jazz, or jazz-oriented styles, could be played beautifully on the archtop instead of the flat-top."

"Personally, I'd like to see some new things explored on the instrument, taking it in some new directions."

"Extremely potent, almost an amplified sound." Scott Chinery

1995—SERIAL #265S

RIBBECKE BLUE MINGIONE

Tom Ribbecke

om Ribbecke is, in his mid-forties, well into his second stint as a full-time luthier. The first ended in 1985, when doctors told him he would never make guitars again.

"I'd opened my shop in San Francisco in 1974, doing repairs and building solid bodies. About ten years later, I developed some sort of acute sensitivity to all kinds of lacquer products. I ended up in the hospital when my lungs shut down. It took me five years to recover."

During his enforced hiatus from guitar making, Ribbecke stayed close to the business by working as a product consultant for Luthier's Mercantile in Healdsburg, California.

A long-time professional musician, Ribbecke first discovered guitars when he was growing up in Brooklyn, New York.

"I was thirteen when my older brother, Larry, returned from MIT with long hair and records by Jimi Hendrix and The Doors. My parents took me to Sears and bought me a Silvertone, which was probably made by Gretsch.

"It was awful. The strings were a quarter-inch above the fretboard, and my fingers would bleed; but I became obsessed with it. It was so awful that I began tinkering with it almost immediately, so that guitar is actually responsible for my fascination with what makes the instrument work and, indirectly, for my career in guitar repair and construction. My first electric was a 335 clone Bruno Conqueror, on which I promptly filed the frets away. I loved the smell of that guitar. It smelled like New York."

Ribbecke, who also teaches lutherie, never apprenticed with anyone. He began teaching himself by going to the library.

"There were maybe three books out there, so I bothered all of my guitar teachers and the local repair people, most of whom were gracious with their information. Also, my father had built ship models that were masterpieces. Just by watching him, I not only learned a lot, but I was empowered to create what I wanted to with my hands.

"I've built about 280 guitars, ninety or so of them arch-tops. Working with my apprentice, Tom Cerletti, I make archtops in three different sizes and many configurations, each taking, on average, about 125 hours to complete.

"The Blue Guitar, which is named for old-time jazz player Andy Mingione, was a special case. Many people suggested that I build my standard guitar, but I took a long walk with my golden retriever and decided to build something new as a true homage to Jimmy D'Aquisto. He was my greatest influence, along with D'Angelico, Lloyd Loar, Stromberg, and Richard Schneider.

"I agonized over the A-hole design and the lines of the pickguard. The Kasha-style bridge was a bit of a stretch. The back and sides are big-leaf western maple, quilted. The top is asymetrical to optimize the tonal energy in the top. The back is quartersawn in the center seam and rolls out more to the slab-sawn orientation on the widest area

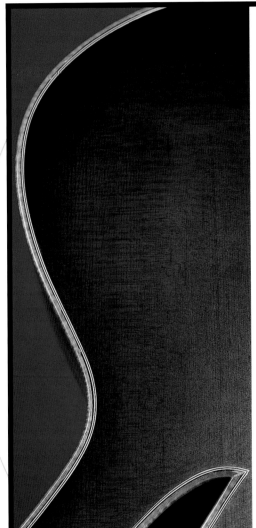

of the back. This is good for broad range tonal coloration— stiff in the center and flexible toward the rim for bass compliance. The top is Sitka spruce—a bit of a departure from Jimmy's work—which is fast to respond. These big guitars are like Cadillacs or Rolls Royces in terms of their response, and the Sitka livens it up a bit for me.

"The neck is bird's-eye maple, and the fittings ebony, with carbon graphite fibre reinforcement of the wooden hinged tailpiece and neck. The binding is flamed curly Koa wood from Hawaii." Perhaps the most unusual feature of this guitar is the carved ebony "sound horn." "I wasn't asked to do a sound port, but I decided to have some fun with the idea anyway. I placed a round ebony monitor hole on the 'driver's side' upper bout, designed to point right at the player's left ear. There is also a folded exponential ebony horn. These horns are fit to, and can be rotated into the sound port.

"We spend years learning about the blend of intuition and science that is great lutherie. We are trained intuitionists. Much of our work is brutal, but this part is an elegant dance with one's own intuition."

"A sound out of heaven, like cherubs playing harps." Scott Chinery

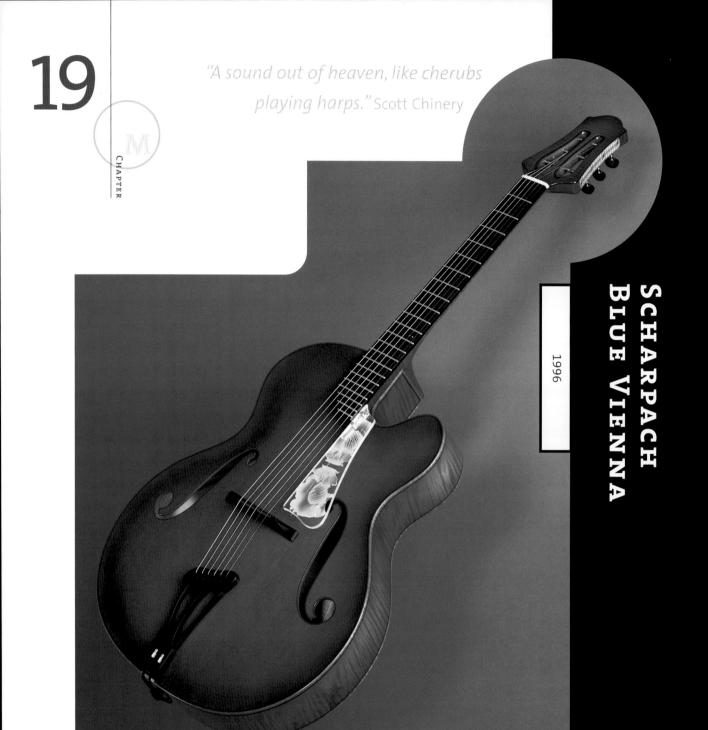

SCHARPACH
BLUE VIENNA

1996

THEO SCHARPACH

T he only European maker in the group, Theo Scharpach, was born in St. Polten, Austria, in 1955. He has made his home in the Netherlands for some years, working as a specialist in restoring seventeenth- and eighteenth-century furniture and clocks before becoming a full-time luthier.

"Like a lot of other guys, I played the guitar during my high school years, but nothing serious. It was not guitar music that attracted me to make guitars, but the guitar itself as an instrument. I never apprenticed with anyone, and there was no particular maker who influenced

Theo Scharpach

my work. I simply tried to get as much information as possible from other players and from books about guitars, violins, pianos, and acoustic research. I also learned a lot about the history of guitar making."

Scharpach is one of the new breed of makers who sees the instrument differently from many of his contemporaries.

"New ideas of guitar making interest me very much. I try to combine old-world craftsmanship with the latest technologic and acoustic information. Sometimes I even do things that seem a bit unusual for a luthier, like making a hurdy-gurdy with a wooden wind pipe organ inside. By delving into the history of the hurdy-gurdy and pipe organ, I found knowledge that helps with my guitars."

In his eighteen years as a working luthier, Scharpach has produced between 250 and 300 instruments. Working alone, he generally takes about six weeks to complete each guitar including varnishing and drying time. As with the other makers, his Blue took some extra effort.

"I've had something like this in mind for about three years—to make an archtop that incorporates everything I have learned in the past twenty years.

"I used wood as dry and old as possible. The bridge is blackened Brazilian rosewood that is more than a hundred years old. The neck is Honduran mahogany with a shell of quartersawn European cello wood 2 mm thick that is heated, shaped, and secured to the neck with hide glue. This construction gives the neck great stability and looks and sounds great.

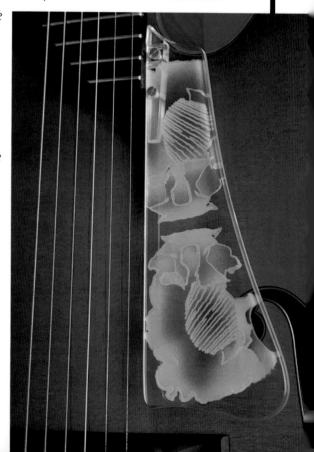

"As you might tell from the pickguard and tuning pegs, I love the style of art deco and art nouveau. I felt the pickguard just had to be transparent so you would be able to look through it at the color blue, which stands for sky and water—the sea. I engraved and sandblasted a sea ornament underneath to enhance the feeling. The material itself is clear polycarbonate with a hardened top layer.

"The tuning pegs were done with machine maker David Rodgers. Although the sides of the head are extremely curved the titanium stringrollers are completely horizontal. This was achieved by countersinking the machines into the head. The knobs are a combination of titanium and black buffalo horn. The sterling silver plates that cover the machines have springs mounted inside to hold the knobs in the correct position.

"I wanted the Blue Vienna to be European in style because people seem to think of archtops as only being from the U.S. I wanted to demonstrate the tradition of hand-carved instruments that for many centuries has had roots deep in European culture. The Blue Vienna should have the excitement *of an old cello more than that of an old Gibson.*"

20

CHAPTER

"Very lutey—medieval—an original strong sound." Steve Howe

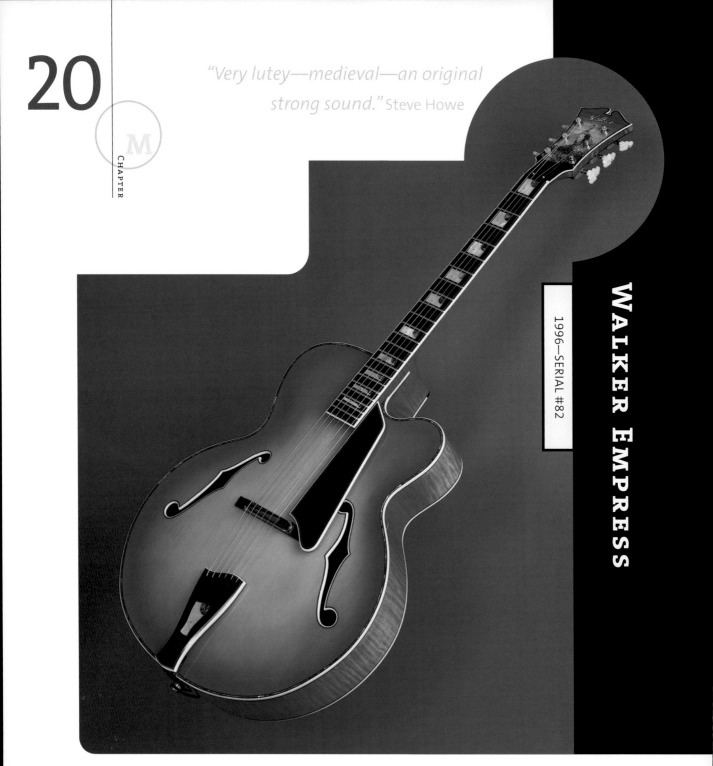

1996—SERIAL #82

WALKER EMPRESS

KIM WALKER

Connecticut luthier Kim Walker has been involved full time in instrument making for twenty-five years.

"I discovered guitars at about fourteen, and at eighteen I bought my first, a Guild D-50. While at the University of Tennessee, I got into roots music, but I always seemed to be more into the guitars themselves—the tone and beauty of them—rather than the playing.

"In 1973, I moved to the Great Smoky mountains to work with Lee Schilling, a former physicist, who was making dulcimers. Shortly afterwards, I started my own business making dulcimers and banjos and repairing guitars. I made my first guitar, a flat-top, in 1974."

In 1979, Walker moved to Nashville to work in the repair shop of fretted-instrument authority, collector, and dealer George Gruhn.

"This was an unparalleled learning opportunity, in terms of working both with highly talented people and unbelievably exciting instruments.

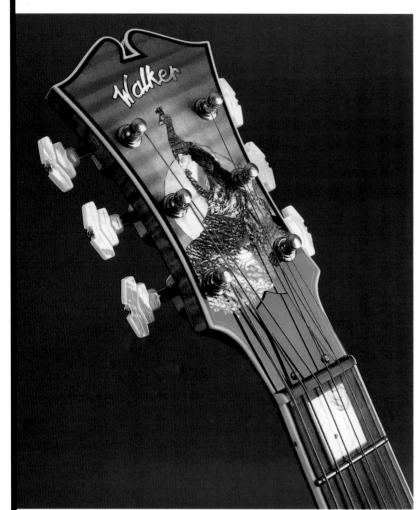

"Some of the instruments I worked on that were influential on my thinking of what makes a good instrument were D'Angelico and D'Aquisto archtops, Lloyd Loar mandolins and Martin flat-tops from the 1920s and 1930s. There were also many examples of what makes a bad instrument."

In 1987, the opportunity arose for Walker to move to Rhode Island in a senior position with Guild Guitars.

"In 1986, I'd gotten involved, through my association with George Gruhn, in making prototypes and doing design work for new Guild models. This led to a job as their R&D and custom shop supervisor. Being involved in all phases of production of some fifty guitars a day is a great way for a maker to get his chops up. During my seven years at Guild, I kept my own shop at home, repairing and building on the side."

"The lightest and most delicately made 18-inch guitar that I've ever seen. The wood is, seemingly, paper thin."

For Walker, who built his first archtop in 1986, the Blue Guitar Project was an "outrageous concept."

"This was a once-in-a-lifetime opportunity to transcend the usual routine of building for the commercial market and cut loose creatively. The planning, design, and gathering of materials for the Blue took four months, and construction another five."

The completed guitar, with its delicate inlay work, is also very light in weight, achieved by combining careful gradations of the plates and using space-age materials for strength. It is, according to Chinery, half the weight of any of the others.

"The lightest and most delicately made 18-inch guitar that I've ever seen. The wood is, seemingly, paper thin."

Perhaps the guitar's most striking feature is the headstock, with its intricate inlay work.

"The headstock design came from studying art deco and art nouveau fashion designs. It just seemed to me that we were dealing with peacock-blue guitars. Also, I knew that the peacock was Bob Benedetto's favorite bird.

"The tail and body are matched green abalone heart. The wings are figured mother-of-pearl; the rising sun, gold mother-of-pearl; the sky, dyed curly maple; and the hill the peacock is sitting on is ebony."

"A sound to match its elegant lines."

Scott Chinery

1996—SERIAL #0140

ZEIDLER JAZZ DELUXE SPECIAL

John Zeidler

F orty-year-old John Zeidler grew up in Flemington, New Jersey, in a house where his father, a cabinetmaker and woodworking teacher, built harpsichords in his basement shop for professional musicians. It was there that John built his first dulcimers and banjos when he was fifteen.

John Zeidler

"While attending high school, I learned to play the guitar. That, in combination with my involvement in wood and metalworking, converged into instrument making. I got a copy of Sloan's Steel String Guitar Construction book and built my first guitar in 1976. As soon as I finished it, I knew that was what I wanted to do as a profession. Fortunately, after graduating, I was able to apprentice for a year with Augustino LoPrinzi, who really gave me the basic training I needed to go out on my own.

"Until I began building full-time, I repaired Martins, Gibsons, D'Angelicos, D'Aquistos, and other makers, all of which influenced the way I build my guitars."

Zeidler has made over a hundred guitars, about thirty mandolins, and many other stringed instruments, including seven violins.

"I specialize in archtop and flat-top acoustic guitars and mandolins. My experience in violin making has influenced my archtop building methods, especially the tap tuning and carving techniques that I learned. I make my own varnishes, which are similar to the kind used on violins, and this has also been significant in the evolution of my instruments."

Like his fellow luthiers, Zeidler added a number of special features to his Blue, which took about eight weeks to build.

"All parts of the head and tailpieces are handmade, rhodium plated, and engraved in a freehand English scroll style with a hand-rubbed, patina finish.

"The end pin and the decorative buttons on the tuner knobs and string posts are hand turned from celluloid tortoise shell.

"The guitar also features select, big-leaf maple back, sides, and neck, with select Adirondack spruce top and X-bracing, a sculptured fingerboard extension, tortoise shell pickguard and binding, and an engraved, rhodium-plated truss-rod cover.

"For me, building a great instrument is an evolving process in which one must blend the best elements of contemporary design and function with timeless traditional craftsmanship.

"Archtop makers are now producing the best and most versatile guitars ever built, converting what was only known as a jazz instrument into something much more. Just as a fine violin sounds great used in classical, folk, jazz, or any other musical form, the modern archtop can be used the same way, with equally great results.

I think it's just a matter of time until players become aware of the modern archtop's versatility."

IT AIN'T OVER TILL THE
FAT LADY SINGS THE BLUES

The Ultra Blue Penetrating Stain #M 520 had barely dried on the twenty-one commissioned Blue Guitars before other archtop luthiers began contacting Scott Chinery about possible additions to the collection. At first reluctant to do anything that might diminish the importance of the original group, Chinery soon realized that the continuation of the Blue Guitar Project could only help to accomplish what he'd intended from the beginning: to promote an awareness of the artistry and versatility of the modern archtop guitar.

"Needless to say, there are a lot of very talented luthiers who were not involved in the project initially. But over time, more instruments will be added to the collection as this renaissance of the archtop guitar continues throughout the world."

Tom Barth

One luthier whose guitar already has been added to the collection is Tom Barth, a maker who specializes in the rapidly grow-ing market for "travel" or "baby" guitars. Carved from a solid block of mahogany, with a spruce top and rosewood bridge, Barth's Baby Blue guitars—there are two versions, a six-string and twelve-string—are the latest in a long line of travel guitars marketed since 1993 under the name TommyHawk.

The origins of this instrument are as unusual as the guitar itself. About ten years ago, Barth repeatedly found himself stuck in New Jersey traffic for hours at a time. A life-long

musician, he kept wishing he could play his guitar while sitting in his car. Voila! The first of more than 170 TommyHawks was born.

"Once I had that guitar with me, I didn't care how long I was stuck in the car."

According to Chinery, the end result is anything but small.

"It's amazing. You get some great sounds out of this tiny little box."

Barth's Baby Blues are seen here with an even smaller Blue Guitar, this one made by British model maker Malcolm Grundy. A gift to Chinery from a fellow collector, Dr. Thomas A. Van Hoose, this perfect replica of the D'Aquisto Centura Deluxe is the only Blue Guitar that can't be played. (Too bad; it seems the perfect size for those crowded rush-hour subway rides.)

The two bottles of blue wine, which may look gimmicky, are actually a legitimate part of the collection. Made by Linda Manzer with labels signed by her fellow luthiers, they form the one part of the collection that is unlikely to be added to.

Jimmy D'Aquisto's final masterpiece, the 1995 Advance

"I decided that if Scott was going to have a big party to celebrate the Blue Guitar collection, it would be appropriate to offer a gift of my homemade wine, with a twist! Originally I searched for some blueberry juice, wanting to go the organic route, but time ran out and I had to go with good ol' blue food color. I had the same problem dying the wine that I had with the blue lacquer on my guitar. If you add blue to a slightly yellow lacquer —-or to wine—it turns green.

Luckily, I had solved this problem with the guitar, so dying the wine *was easy.*"

"BLUE DAWN" by Leslie Jean-Bart

AFTERWORD

TAKING THE ARCHTOP TO THE MILLENNIUM AND BEYOND

So that's life, then: things as they are?

It picks its way on the blue guitar.

A million people on one string?

And all their manner in the thing,

And all their manner, right and wrong,

And all their manner, weak and strong?

The feelings crazily, craftily call,

Like a buzzing of flies in autumn air,

And that's life then: things as they are,

This buzzing of the blue guitar.

Excerpt from "Man with the Blue Guitar," by Wallace Stevens

"The resurgence of the archtop over the last ten years is unprecedented in the history of the guitar. The archtop has grown from a big band rhythm instrument to a guitar that is now used for virtually every type of music. The luthiers of today are pushing the envelope of archtop design further than was thought possible by their predecessors; and, in many cases, they are building the best archtop guitars in the history of the instrument.

"The Blue Guitars collection is the culmination of almost a century of design, innovation, and craftsmanship. This outstanding group of instruments clearly illustrates the state of the craft as we near the end of the century in which the archtop originated." Larry Acunto, *20th Century Guitar*

The four-hundred-plus-year history of the guitar, from the earliest descendants of the lute to the final masterpieces of Jimmy D'Aquisto and the work of today's innovators, has been one of evolutionary rather than revolutionary change. Even the great achievement of Orville Gibson, replacing the instrument's standard flat top with an arched top based on violin design principles, was built upon the past. For today's best archtop luthiers, exemplified by those in the Blue Guitar collection, the challenge is to continue that evolutionary progression. It's been quite a while since Orville Gibson put the "arch" in archtop, so what's next?

"When it comes to the archtop, I've never thought there were any limitations to what it could do, no golden rule about right or wrong. The archtop to me has got everything. Certainly, when you want your own personality to come through, that's the guitar you should do it on." Steve Howe

THE PLAYERS

Jimmy D'Aquisto believed the archtop was more suited to many different types of music than the flat-top and had, in fact, already moved well away from the more traditional philosophy typified by his mentor, John D'Angelico. He left behind a tantalizing glimpse into the future as he saw it with his final model, the 1995 Advance.

The Chinery Collection

Featuring four removable sound baffles in the top plate, it offered the player eighteen different choices of tonality and volume. The extra-strength *X*-bracing used to compensate for the larger soundholes also gives the instrument tremendous power. The luthiers profiled in this book have their own views on where the instrument is going, as does Scott Chinery. *"The archtop* is vastly different than it was fifty years ago. Then it had a big, brassy kind of sound, designed to cut through a big band. Today, it's a much more open instrument, much more versatile. There are a lot of new players using the archtop who, just a few years ago, would only have used a flat-top."

Bob Benedetto, the dean of this generation of luthiers, has his own take on the subject: "*Whether or not the archtop is still evolving remains to be seen. I don't think anybody's going to pull a rabbit out of a hat. Certainly not every new feature or appointment with claims of superiority can be taken seriously. I believe a maker should be in touch with players.*

"*The player is the maker's link to reality; and from a player's point of view, the archtop should feel, look, and sound a certain way. If we deviate too much from that, it becomes a different instrument.*"

Nashville's Jim Triggs is of a similar mind.

"*I believe the archtop has peaked in the short term. There will always be new people coming up with new designs, but it's going to be hard to get that vintage sound without building them 'the way they used to.'*"

One of the factors affecting the way archtops will be made in the future is the decreasing availability of fine tone wood. Some luthiers, like Bill Comins, think this problem can only be solved by using other materials.

"*As resources become more scarce, guitar makers and consumers will have to learn to appreciate alternative woods and materials. We must continue to refine our craft both intuitively and through technology. The use of the computer in design and construction already has opened many new doors. There are so many stones yet unturned.*"

Like many of his contemporaries, John Buscarino takes his lead from the players themselves.

"*I think archtops are being built more acoustically than they used to be, and I see that trend continuing. I also see more emphasis on electronics and computers. It's always hard to say where and how archtop building will evolve; but, as the music changes and the players come up with new twists and more innovative styles, I notice that's when I start changing my thinking about how I build guitars.*"

Buscarino's emphasis on what the player wants is echoed by all the luthiers, regardless of their philosophical bent. Theo Scharpach explains:

"In my opinion, the new type of archtop should sound much closer in character to a nylon-stringed than a steel-stringed instrument. It should not have that mid-range sound preferred by rhythm players in a big band, but be more subtle, with a warm and colorful sound like a classical guitar. Of course, there is no one solution to making the ultimate guitar, because every player will ask for different possibilities."

John Monteleone cautions that "You can't get away from certain parameters.

"You have to be careful not to design an instrument that competes with itself. If we look at other modern artists—Picasso for example—they are well-schooled, well-grounded in the basics, and that groundwork becomes the foundation for innovation. Design innovations have to warrant their inclusion. Sometimes less is more. If the player can't or won't play a new guitar design, then it's a dead end."

The truth of the matter is that it takes two people to complete a guitar, the luthier and the player for whom it is made.

"Like quite a lot of players, I don't really know very much about guitars. When I'm playing an instrument that speaks back to me with the sound I have in my head, then there's no effort in playing. I don't mean just physically, but in getting my musical ideas out through the instrument. So I don't always ask myself deep questions about a particular guitar. It's more like: Wow, this guitar is great. It's a kind of mystery having an instrument with no barriers to your communication with it. Guitar makers could probably explain it. It's funny, but when you meet a guitar maker after you've played their guitar, you already have an idea about them from their instrument."
Martin Taylor

According to Linda Manzer, "There is an elusive quality that an archtop has that no other guitar has. It is partly the sound, but also the way the archtop can represent the player's musical vision more completely when it is played by someone who loves it. That truly is the magic, and that's why I love them. As for the future, I find most design changes I make to instruments come from players' requests to find 'their' instrument.

"So as long as there is an open-minded luthier and an inquisitive player, there will be change. You can count on it."

Coda

"There are many who ridicule the guitar
and its sound. But if they think it over,
they will discover that the guitar is
the most favorable instrument of our time."

Luis de Briceno, 1626

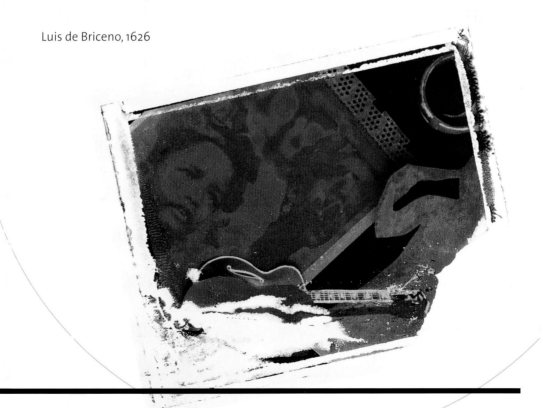

"INDIGO MOOD" by Leslie Jean-Bart

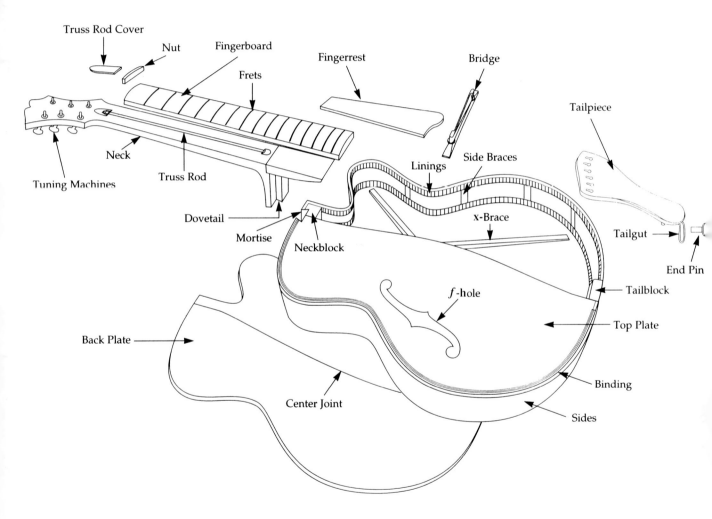

Exploded view of an archtop guitar from the book *Making an Archtop Guitar* by Robert Benedetto. (Copyright © 1994, Robert Benedetto)

Truss Rod Cover

Nut

Fingerboard

Frets

Fingerrest

Bridge

Tailpiece

Neck

Truss Rod

Tuning Machines

Linings

Side Braces

Dovetail

Mortise

Neckblock

x-Brace

Tailgut

End Pin

f-hole

Tailblock

Back Plate

Top Plate

Center Joint

Binding

Sides

THE PLAYERS

GEORGE BENSON

George Benson has been performing professionally for more than forty years—as a child rhythm and blues artist, as a master jazz guitarist, and finally, as a contemporary multitalented player, vocalist, and composer whose record sales are counted in the millions. He has recorded with Miles Davis, Herbie Hancock, Freddie Hubbard and Quincy Jones. In 1976 his *Breezin'* became the first jazz recording to sell four million albums and go platinum. Benson's knowledge of the guitar as a player is augmented by a twenty-year association with the Japanese manufacturer Ibanez, for whom he has designed five instruments, including the GB20 archtop.

STEVE HOWE

Steve Howe first gained fame as a member of Tomorrow and the mega-rock groups Yes and Asia. Called "the thinking man's guitar hero," Howe combines his recording and playing career with activities as composer, arranger, guitar historian, and collector. His book *The Steve Howe Guitar Collection,* coauthored with Tony Bacon, was published in 1994. Howe and Martin Taylor recently collaborated on an album featuring a selection of historically significant guitars from the Chinery Collection, including nineteen Blue Guitars.

MARTIN TAYLOR

Scotland's Martin Taylor has been playing guitar since the age of four. A ten-year association with legendary violinist Stephane Grappelli introduced Taylor to the jazz world, through appearances at festivals and concert halls around the globe. Taylor's first solo album, *A Tribute to Art Tatum,* was released in 1984. Called "lyrical and commanding, a technical marvel" by *Downbeat Magazine,* Taylor has collaborated with such outstanding musicians as Chet Atkins, Barney Kessel, David Grisman, Bill Wyman, and Yehudi Menuhin.

BLUE GUITAR—CONTACT LIST

THE CHINERY COLLECTION—908-244-0676
PO Box 1371 Toms River, NJ 08754—www.chinery.com

LUTHIERS The names appearing in parentheses represent some of the players who use instruments made by that particular luthier.

TOM BARTH—201-366-6611 Tom Barth's Music
Box 291 West Clinton St. Dover, NJ 07801 (Allan Woody/
Tony Mottola/Joe Goryeb)

ROBERT BENEDETTO—717-223-0883 (7711 FAX) RR1 Box 1347
E. Stroudsburg, PA 18301—http://benedetto-guitars.com
(Howard Alden/John & Bucky Pizzarelli/Frank Vignola/
Jimmy Bruno/Adrian Ingram)

JOHN BUSCARINO—813-586-4992 (581-4535 FAX)
9075-B 130th Ave, Largo, FL 33773—(Ron Affif/Steve Morse/
Paul Bollenback)

MARK CAMPELLONE—401-351-4229 725 Branch Ave. Box 125
Providence, RI 02904 (Frank Potenza/Adrian Ingram)

BILL COLLINGS—512-288-7776 (6045 FAX) 11025 Signal Hill Dr.
Austin, TX 78737 (Steve Miller/Lyle Lovett/Andy
Summers/Eddie Van Halen/Joan Baez)

BILL COMINS—215-784-0314 PO Box 611 Willow Grove, PA
19001 (Trefor Owen/Joe Sgro/Bob Denardo)

JAMES DALE/D'LECO—405-524-0448 PO Box 60432
Oklahoma City, OK 73146-0432 (Jimmy Ponder)

FENDER CUSTOM SHOP—909-734-7739 (3357 FAX)
Fender Musical Instruments Corp. 1163-A Pomona Rd.
Corona, CA 91720 (Eric Clapton/Bonnie Raitt/
James Burton/Buddy Guy/Steve Cropper)

GIBSON CUSTOM SHOP—615-871-4500 (9517 FAX) Gibson
Guitar Corp. 1818 Elmhill Pike, Nashville, TN 37210 (Barney
Kessel/Howard Roberts/Larry Carlton/Al DeMeola)

STEVE GRIMES—808-878-2076 PO Box 537
Kula, HI 96790 (George Benson/Steve Miller/Kenny
Rankin/Walter Becker/Earl Klugh/Kenny Loggins)

BILL HOLLENBECK—217-732-6933 (2053 FAX) 160 Half Moon
St. Lincoln, IL 62656 (Martin Taylor)

MARK LACEY—615-952-3045 (4626 FAX) PO Box 24646
Nashville, TN 37202 (Rick Neilson/Leo Kottke/Bon Jovi)

LINDA MANZER—416-927-1539 (8233 FAX) 65 Metcalf St.
Toronto, ONT M4X 1R9 Canada e-mail: manzer@interlog.com
—http://www.scsi.org/manzer.guitars (Pat Metheny/Carlos
Santana/Milton Nascimento)

TED MEGAS—415-822-3100 (1454 FAX) 1070 Van Dyke
San Francisco, CA 94124 (Richard Johnson/Bill McCormick)

JOHN MONTELEONE—516-277-3620 (3639 FAX) PO Box 52
Islip, NY 11751 (Mitch Seidman/Laurie Stewart/Paul Ritchie/
Don Sternberg)

BRAD NICKERSON—413-586-8521 (584-6027 FAX)
8 Easthampton Rd. Northampton, MA 01060
(Agostino DiGiorgio/Johannes Hummel/David Shoup)

BOZO PODUNAVAC—941-474-3288 (473-8221 FAX)
2340 Englewood Rd Englewood, FL 34223 (Leo Kottke/
Peter Lang/John Fahey)

TOM RIBBECKE—707-433-3778 PO Box 1581
Santa Rosa, CA 95402 e-mail: tom@ribbecke.com
(Seal/Pete Snell/Pat Smith/Howard Krive)

THEO SCHARPACH—011-31-497-541278 Achterste Aa 14 5571
VE Bergeyk The Netherlands (Steve Howe/Al DiMeola)

JIM TRIGGS—615-391-5844 3036 Jenry Drive
Nashville, TN 37214 (Mundell Lowe/Steve Miller/Pat Martino/
Alan Jackson/Ranger Doug)

KIM WALKER—860-599-8753 314 Pendleton Road North
Stonington, CT 06359 (Loy Smith/Ron Rothman/Andy Smith)

JOHN ZEIDLER—215-271-6858 1441 S. Broad St.
Philadelphia, PA 19147 e-mail: jrzeidler@aol.com—
http://www.cyboard.com/ent/zeidler.html (Steve
Obermeyer/Pat Mercuri/John McGann)

BIBLIOGRAPHY

BOOKS

THE CHINERY COLLECTION: 150 YEARS OF AMERICAN GUITARS by Scott Chinery and Tony Bacon
Outline Press, London— © 1996

GIBSON GUITARS: 100 YEARS OF AN AMERICAN ICON by Walter Carter
General Publishing Group, Inc., Santa Monica, CA— © 1994

MAKING AN ARCHTOP GUITAR by Robert Benedetto
Centerstream Publishing, Anaheim Hills, CA— © 1994

ACOUSTIC GUITARS AND OTHER FRETTED INSTRUMENTS by George Gruhn and Walter Carter
GPI Books, San Francisco— © 1993

AMERICAN GUITARS: AN ILLUSTRATED HISTORY by Tom Wheeler
HarperCollins Publishers, New York— © 1992

THE ULTIMATE GUITAR BOOK by Tony Bacon
Alfred A. Knopf, Inc., New York— © 1991

THE GUITAR: FROM THE RENAISSANCE TO THE PRESENT DAY by Harvey Turnbull
The Bold Strummer Ltd., Westport, CT— © 1974, 1991

THE HISTORY AND DEVELOPMENT OF THE AMERICAN GUITAR by Ken Achard
The Bold Strummer Ltd., Westport, CT— © 1990

PERIODICALS

20TH CENTURY GUITAR	**GUITAR PLAYER**
ACOUSTIC GUITAR	**VINTAGE GUITAR**
JUST JAZZ GUITAR	**AMERICAN LUTHERIE**